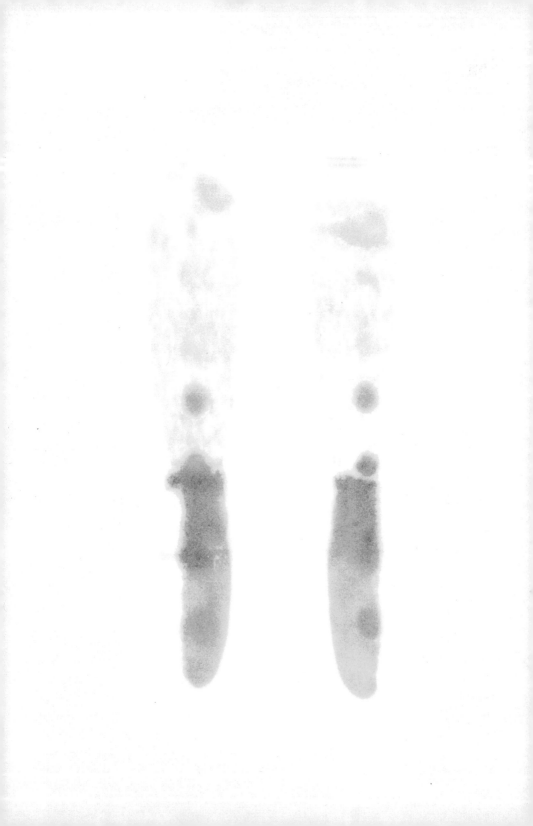

CONSPICUOUS CONSUMPTION

CONSPICUOUS CONSUMPTION

A Study of Exceptional Consumer Behavior

ROGER S. MASON

St. Martin's Press　　　New York

Library of Congress Cataloging in Publication Data

Mason, Roger S.

  Conspicuous consumption

  1. Consumers.   I. Title
HC79.C6M37   658.8'342   80-16196
ISBN 0-312-16424-6

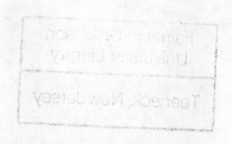

ISBN 0-312-16424-6

Contents

Acknowledgements

My thanks are due to the many colleagues and
friends with whom I discussed this work and
who offered much valuable comment and
constructive criticism; to Margaret Blease for
all her efforts in preparing the final manuscript;
and to Marnie, Sarah and Christopher for their
patience and support over many years.

Roger S. Mason

Introduction

Theories of demand and of consumer preference formation are based on the proposition that all goods and services are wanted and purchased for the utility they offer to the buyer. Each consumer good is seen to offer a bundle of utilities which is compared with those of competing commodities by potential buyers and which directly decides the level of demand generated for the product in question. Whilst this interpretation of product value and consumer behaviour gives a general explanation of the buying process it says little or nothing about the nature of 'utilities' being sought by consumers in making their purchase decisions.

The great majority of purchases are made for the direct, personal satisfaction that product consumption offers to the buyer and utility measurement is essentially a self-centred process in which the personal preferences of the individual or buying group are alone responsible for the decision to buy. General theories of product utility are necessarily based on this pattern of 'exclusive' personal preference formation but can not accommodate those exceptional forms of consumer behaviour in which the buyer's assessment of third-party opinion and reaction to his proposed purchase becomes the major factor in his decision to buy. In such cases, product utility derives not from personal consumption in a literal sense but from the value placed on the purchase by other individuals or social groups whose opinions are of significant importance to the buyer.

One such form of exceptional behaviour—conspicuous consumption—is concerned primarily with the ostentatious display of wealth. Motivated by a desire to impress others with the ability to pay particularly high prices for prestige products, it is a form of consumption which is inspired by the social rather than by the economic or physiological utility of products. In its pure form, when the consumer is influenced in his decision to buy only by a wish or need to display purchasing power, the direct utility of the commodity he purchases—that is, its utility in use—is of no interest. Satisfaction is derived from audience reaction not to the positive attributes of the good or service in question but to the wealth displayed by the purchaser in securing the product for consumption. Consequently, the cost of purchase—or product price—becomes the only factor of any significance to the buyer.

Conspicuous consumption is no recent phenomenon. Evidence of such behaviour can be found in the earliest societies and the economic extravagances and excesses of many individuals and social groups have been well documented. Indeed, the cumulative effect of these excesses has often been such that the conspicuous economic display of privileged elites has acted as a catalyst for radical social and political changes which have transformed many societies. In more recent years, a combination of factors has made 'pure' consupicuous consumption increasingly rare but it has undoubtedly survived—often in modified form—as an economic and social reality. Status and prestige considerations still play a significant part in shaping preferences for many products which are purchased ostensibly for direct utility but which are 'visible' to others either at the point of purchase or consumption. Present-day snob and bandwagon effects (q.v.) are derivatives of conspicuous consumption and can have a considerable influence on consumer choice and demand. In short, conspicuous display has been adapted to changing economic and social circumstances and can still be a significant force today even in those societies which have rejected or suppressed it in its more extreme form. It certainly continues to provide the stimulus—directly or indirectly—for much economic and social reform. This present work, however, focuses not on the wider social and political debate but on conspicuous consumption itself and on the nature and incidence of such behaviour over time.

Notwithstanding the importance of conspicuous consumption in social, political and economic terms, little real attention has been given to the subject in the last fifty years. It was first examined in any detail by Thorstein Veblen in his book *The Theory of the Leisure Class* published in 1899. However, Veblen himself was more directly concerned with opening a discussion on the inadequacies of the American system of finance capitalism and did not research specifically into the conspicuous economic display which was, for him, a particular feature of the society on which his political and economic critique was centred. His work on conspicuous consumption was subjective and none of his claims concerning the underlying motivations of such behaviour was supported by original research. Nevertheless, his contribution laid the foundation for further research which since that time has been remarkable only by its absence.

Conspicuous economic display would appear to be motivated primarily by status and prestige considerations and in recent years a considerable body of knowledge has been developed on the structure of different status systems and on the social psychology of groups. At the same time, no research work has specifically explored the relationship between status, group psychology and conspicuous consumption. The fundamental need has not been to define status as such but to examine the importance of wealth and wealth display as a means to status improvement and to match patterns of conspicuous consumption with a society's status system.

Of the few conspicuous consumption studies carried out to date, all have accepted status considerations as the dominant motive force behind such behaviour but the relationship between a given type of conspicuous expenditure and the specific status goal it seeks to achieve has not been examined in any detail. In fact, to make any progress it is important to recognise that conspicuous consumption may be undertaken for many different reasons—mostly although not exclusively status-directed—and that particular objectives will in large part determine the form such consumption will take. Distinctions need to be made between ostentatious display intended to secure new status gains and that intended to preserve and protect a level of status already achieved; between expenditures directed at 'vertical' (between-group) gains and those seeking 'horizontal' (within-group) objectives; and between voluntary and compulsory display in the interests of status consolidation.

One possible explanation for the failure to examine the many status-display relationships which can exist is that the pattern of conspicuous consumption observed by Veblen at the end of the nineteenth century has been too easily accepted as typical of all conspicuous economic behaviour. The overwhelming motive force behind the ostentatious display of the 'Gilded Age' in the United States was an uncomplicated desire on the part of American 'nouveaux riches' to buy social status and the conspicuous behaviour of that age has, since Veblen, often been taken as representative of most if not all other pure conspicuous consumption. However, there is considerable evidence to show that the American experience from 1860–1910 was perhaps atypical and should not serve as a standard against which other observations are judged and categorised. Research, therefore, can not take Veblen's work as definitive but must more properly include his observations only as part of a more broadly based analysis. In practice the focal point of all research efforts to date has been on the so-called 'Veblen Effect'—an expression which itself reveals the narrow definition often given to the subject.

Whatever the true reasons for the obvious lack of research effort, our knowledge and understanding of conspicuous consumption—both in social and economic terms—is today superficial and far from satisfactory. No cumulative evidence has been assembled to confirm or refute subjective claims that such behaviour is to be observed at all stages of social and economic development; many field researchers have recorded instances of conspicuous economic display but these observations have not been 'clustered' and placed in their different social, political and economic contexts; no research has been carried out to establish if and how conspicuous consumption itself changes in response to changes in the socio-economic environment; and Veblen's claim that such behaviour can be observed at all social and economic levels within a particular society and is not to be associated only with privileged (i.e. rich) elites remains unsubstantiated.

Specialist research into the subject has given us a highly fragmented and often inconsistent picture of conspicuous economic display and it is clear that a quite explicit multi-disciplinary approach needs to be taken if further progress is to be made. In particular, far more information is needed with respect to the socio-economic conditions which motivate such behaviour.

Research into the subject can never be easy. Conspicuous consumption is a form of economic behaviour to which individuals will not admit. By acknowledging that a particular purchase decision is undertaken primarily for status or other 'social' purposes the conspicuous consumer loses any advantage which such consumption may otherwise afford him. At the same time, the purchase and consumption must by definition be conspicuous and this gives us the opportunity to identify such behaviour within many societies and to match observed patterns of conspicuous consumption with the social and economic conditions under which they occur.

The analysis which follows does not attempt to offer a comprehensive theory of conspicuous consumption. It does, however, seek to explain the theoretical basis for such behaviour and proposes a research framework within which further work can most usefully proceed. Evidence of the nature and incidence of conspicuous economic display is examined within this proposed frame of reference and an attempt made to explain the many patterns of conspicuous consumption which are identified and described. Above all, the work offers a more formal treatment of this exceptional form of consumer behaviour and invites both critical reaction and a greater research interest in the subject.

1 Conspicuous consumption in economic and social thought

The existence and consequences of conspicuous consumption had been recognised long before publication of Veblen's *The Theory of Leisure Class* at the end of the nineteenth century. Luxury consumption at the time of the Roman Empire was seen as a problem so serious that sumptuary laws were introduced to suppress it. Throughout medieval times such ostentatious display was condemned primarily for moral reasons (it was considered sinful in the eyes of God to indulge in excessive consumption) but also because ostentation was seen to be a possible threat to a set of class relations which the medieval world considered it important to preserve. Up to 1600, legislation had at various times been used unsuccessfully throughout Europe to forbid the consumption of everything from clothes to food.

The case against ostentatious economic behaviour had traditionally been based on ethical considerations prior to 1600 but after this date the issue was transposed from the moral to the economic sphere. Lack of personal frugality was now condemned not only because it disturbed a class organisation of society but because it weakened the productive ability of a nation. It was held responsible for increasing imports and weakening home markets, for having adverse effects upon the individual as a producer and for discouraging thrift and industry.[1] During this period, luxury and extravagance continued to be regarded as cancerous social and economic diseases. Rather than as an indicator of a flourishing economy, 'excessive' consumption was seen as a sympton of economic decay.[2] It was felt to be particularly dangerous to allow the 'middle or lower classes of men' to indulge in such behaviour and many observers

1

therefore argued that it was the responsibility of those of higher station to set a good example and lead frugal lives themselves.[3]

A significant change in attitude towards luxury consumption began to emerge in the last quarter of the seventeenth century when for the first time the substantial benefits associated with ostentatious levels of consumption were being recognised. Demand for luxury goods necessarily meant more employment for those who had the skills to provide them. Given a policy of import control, it was argued, an economy could only benefit from such activity. Furthermore, countries who had actively suppressed conspicuous consumption were almost invariably poor, a fact attributed to the tendency of such legislation to repress industry and innovation.[4] After 1700, therefore, a reasonable demand for luxuries was increasingly seen as a benefit rather than as a handicap to economic and social progress and craftsmen were encouraged to supply this limited market with the goods that it required.

The early critics and advocates of luxury consumption had concentrated their attention on the consequences of such behaviour both for the individual and for the society in which he lived—consequences measured in moral and economic terms. Before 1750, few writers had given any consideration to the actual motivations underlying ostentatious economic display and to the possible objectives being pursued by the individual who chose to use his discretionary income and wealth in such a manner. The generally accepted explanation of such behaviour was one of uncomplicated self-indulgence—a wish to maximise personal pleasure in the consumption of expensive goods and services.[5]

John Locke was one of the few observers who saw something more substantial in seventeenth century extravagence and challenged the view that utility derived solely from personal consumption of the goods in question. In particular, he was among the first to recognise the special importance of price in the context of ostentatious display and argued that 'fashion is for the most part nothing but the ostentation of riches and therefore the high price of what serves to that rather increases than lessens its vent'.[6] For the first time, consideration was given to the possibility that under the right social conditions demand and price could be positively correlated and that price could be seen as a positive product attribute. However, whilst it was recognised that such attitudes to money and to consumption could exist, no attempts were made to explain why social acceptance, status and prestige were considered important by the individual and why conspicuous consumption was accepted by many as a means of achieving such objectives.

The relatively dismissive discussion and treatment of conspicuous consumption was effectively ended by Adam Smith who devoted a far greater effort to exploring this particular aspect of consumer behaviour. Smith argued firstly that people had moved from the simple gratification of bodily appetites to the satisfaction of social and cultural needs, from physical to social survival. Faced with this need for social approval, the individual therefore needed to find a way to establish and consolidate his personal status and prestige within the community.[7] Smith believed there was 'empirical proof'[8] to show that social position (in the eighteenth century at least) was determined in practice by an individual's accumulated wealth and saw the need to display personal wealth as a fundamental necessity for those seeking status within society. Given this need, the conspicuous consumption of goods and services was seen as providing an ideal opportunity for wealth display in the interests of social advancement.

Smith saw ostentatious consumption as a social action, an attempt by men to acquire the symbols they needed to identify their status in society. The struggle for wealth and consumer goods was simply a struggle for prestige, position and power.[9] In particular, he argued that in the 'commercial' societies which had grown out of the Middle Ages, wealth had always to be converted into consumables before it became effective as an instrument of status improvement. The rich needed to purchase many goods simply because they were expensive and therefore were 'objects for which nobody can afford to pay but themselves'.[10]

Three interesting conclusions are drawn in the Smith analysis. Firstly, conspicuous consumption was seen as a relatively recent (i.e. eighteenth century) phenomenon made necessary only by commercialisation of society and by the increasingly 'sophisticated' economic and social system of the time. Secondly, it was considered a necessary social phenomenon because the inequality of wealth could become a source of social peace and continuity only when it was transformed into ostentation. Ostentatious consumption was therefore not only proper in a stratified society but indeed was functionally essential in ensuring the power of the oligarchy.[11] Finally, the ostentatious display of the rich was seen as a good thing in that it gave incentives to the poor to work hard in the hope of emulating their masters.[12]

Overall, Smith's attitude to conspicuous consumption was highly ambivalent. Whilst arguing that such behaviour was both necessary and desirable, he also proposed intervention by fiscal devices to alter the pattern of expenditures in favour of investment and away from luxury consumption. However, the contradiction was recognised for, while never explicitly developing the point, he conceded that a potential conflict could exist between the need for productive investment to secure economic growth and the equally important need, in his eyes, to maintain social stability through the conspicuous consumption of the rich.

Adam Smith's works came to dominate economic thought after their publication, but it is unfortunate that his views on conspicuous economic display were taken no further. The next contribution of any value came in the mid-nineteenth century from John Rae, a Canadian, who argued that there was one very simple motivation for the excesses and luxury expenditures of his own times—that of vanity.[13] Rae defined luxury as 'the expenditure occasioned by the passion of vanity . . . the mere desire of superiority over others, without reference to the merit of that superiority' and went on 'things to which vanity seems most readily to apply itself are those to which the use of consumption is most apparent, and of which the effects are most difficult to discriminate. Articles of which the consumption is not conspicuous are incapable of gratifying this passion.'[14]

Vanity, Rae believed, was such a powerful influence that consumers whose income increased in real terms would spend more money on luxuries so that their total expenditures would still take the same share of their greater wealth. However, it is interesting to note that this interpretation of ostentatious economic display is in marked contrast to that of Smith. Rae did not recognise any legitimate or understandable social need for conspicuous consumption and his claim that such behaviour was inspired purely by self-indulgence had more in common with the pre-1750 view of conspicuous display. Furthermore, he argued that—irrespective of the social and economic environment in which men live—increases in conspicuous consumption are an inevitable consequence of increases not in discretionary but in total income; individuals therefore attempt to allocate a constant proportion of their overall wealth to ostentatious economic display rather than increase the proportion as wealth increases and vice-versa.

The proposition that vanity rather than social status lay at the heart of conspicuous consumption was broadly accepted by Alfred Marshall who himself gave some limited attention to the subject.[15] Marshall, however, took a moral, reformist view of such behaviour and suggested that it was in the interests of both the individual and society at large to reduce the overall level of economic display. He acknowledged that the desire for distinction through consumption 'comes with us from the cradle and never leaves us till we go to the grave' and believed this desire to be 'the most powerful of human passions'.[16] But at the same time he saw a real need to suppress such self-display and to redirect ostentatious behaviour into public goods:

> There is some misuse of wealth in all ranks of society . . . even among the artisans of England, and perhaps still more in new countries, there are signs of the growth of that unwholesome desire for wealth as a means of display which has been the chief bane of the well-to-do classes in every civilised country. Laws against luxury have been futile; but it would be a gain if the moral sentiment of the community could induce people to avoid all sorts of display of individual wealth. There are indeed true and worthy pleasures to be got from wisely-ordered magnificence: but they are at their best when free

from any taint of personal vanity on the one side and envy on the other; as they are when they centre round public buildings, public parks, public collections of fine arts and public games and amusements.[17]

Soon after Marshall's *Principles of Economics* appeared in 1890, Thorstein Veblen published *The Theory of the Leisure Class*—a study which has since become the classic analysis of ostentatious economic display.[18] In his book, Veblen introduced the specific term 'conspicuous consumption' for the first time and attempted a detailed explanation of the nature and incidence of such behaviour.

The Theory of the Leisure Class was never intended exclusively as a commentary on conspicuous display. Veblen sub-titled the work 'An Economic Study of Institutions' and was primarily concerned with discussing the place and value of the leisure class as an economic factor in 'modern' (i.e. late nineteenth century) life. However, in attempting to explain the economic and social behaviour of this group, he found it necessary to identify and explore the phenomenon of conspicuous consumption in order to advance the central theoretical premises of his book.

Veblen was concerned, amongst other things, with what he considered to be the socially unacceptable levels of conspicuous consumption which were much in evidence in the United States towards the end of the nineteenth century. The motivation for such behaviour, he believed, could only be derived from the social importance—in terms of status and prestige—which was being given to the display of superior individual ownership and wealth. On this assumption, one with which Adam Smith would not have argued, he then attempted a more comprehensive social and anthropological explanation of ostentatious economic display. His subsequent thesis remains a major contribution to the subject and must now be examined in some detail.

In primitive, predatory societies, Veblen argued, competition is not between individual members of a particular group but between the group and its 'enemies'. War booty and trophies serve as tangible evidence of prowess and as prima facie evidence of successful aggression—aggression itself being recognised as the principal source of group status. However, status is seen as a collective attribute and the possession of trophies tends to be group or tribal possession rather than that intended to reflect on any one member's individual status.[19]

For so long as group interests dominate individual interests, then no significant internal rivalry for social status can develop. Eventually, however, the more successful men in any particular group seek to put their own particular prowess in evidence by exhibiting some durable

5

results of their own exploits. Individuals then begin to take a personal credit for the trophies they have accumulated and a system of private property is quickly established. At the most basic level, individual ownership of women and slaves is important but possession is subsequently extended to the products of their industry and so there arises the ownership of things as well as of persons. In this way, a consistent system of property in goods is gradually installed—a system which increasingly differentiates between individuals on the basis of wealth rather than on aggression and fighting skills.[20]

(Veblen acknowledged that possession could be seen separately as an essential factor in the struggle for survival in all societies and was intended, certainly at subsistence levels, to secure basic physical comforts and necessities. However, he believed that the dominant incentive to ownership was unrelated to the subsistence minimum and 'was from the outset the invidious distinction attaching to wealth').

The possession of wealth gains in relative importance and effectiveness as a customary basis of repute and esteem as societies become increasingly industrialised and as the decline in predatory warfare reduces the opportunity to display status through physical aggression. In essence, a new form of 'aggression' develops—based on the competitive accumulation of goods through success at work. Possession of goods and property becomes a prerequisite in seeking a reputable standing in the community; ownership is seen as an indicator of industrial effectiveness and work-efficiency. In other words, individual wealth is taken as a legitimate measure of a person's contribution and value to the community.

Wealth is therefore given social recognition primarily because it is accepted as 'proof' of industrial commitment and effort but this link between work and reward as the basis of status-conference becomes increasingly weakened. Eventually, wealth comes to be recognised in its own right as a sufficient reason for awarding status, thus putting pressure on individuals not to display their work-contribution to society but to accumulate money, goods and services by whatever means this can be achieved:

> It becomes indispensable to accumulate, to acquire property, in order to retain one's good name. When accumulated goods have in this way become the accepted badge of efficiency, the possession of wealth presently assumes the character of an independent and definitive basis of esteem. . . The possession of wealth, which was at the outset valued simply as an evidence of efficiency, becomes, in popular apprehension, itself a meritorious act. Wealth is now itself intrinsically honourable and confers honour on its possessor.[21]

Man's propensity for achievement within society therefore becomes more and more 'financial' as societies evolve and develop and pecuniary

comparison with others becomes the conventional end of action.
comes to be measured solely in terms of wealth and the pr
achievement is motivated by a clear need for what Veblen des
'pecuniary emulation'.[22] As the possession of property and goods there
fore becomes important to building and maintaining self-respect, each
individual in a community feels a need to own as much as his near socio-
economic neighbours. A major problem, however, is that the process
must be a continuing one. Standards keep rising and what was once an
exceptional possession rapidly becomes widely owned. This means that
people tend to strive continually to make new acquisitions but are
repeatedly frustrated as increases in the overall standard of wealth combine to reduce the perceived 'value' of a given level of ownership and
fuels a further round of wealth accumulation based on the new
standard.[23]

This ratchet effect on pecuniary emulation may be accentuated by a
further factor. Veblen claimed that wealth accumulation is often intended not only to equal or match the wealth standard of the rest of
the community but to exceed it in the hope of securing a status ranking
which is well above the average. If and when the individual has reached
what may be called the normal pecuniary standard of the community
or of his class in the community he may then strive 'to place a wider
and ever-widening pecuniary interval between himself and this average
standard. Invidious comparison can never become so favourable to the
individual making it that he would not gladly rate himself still higher
relative to his competitors in the struggle for pecuniary reputability . . .
no general increase of the community's wealth can make any approach
to satiating this need, the ground of which is the desire of everyone to
excel everyone else in the accumulation of goods.'[24]

Veblen sought to establish that social evolution inevitably creates
conditions in which the accumulation of wealth becomes the necessary
means to short term and long term status recognition. However, he also
argued that accumulated wealth is of itself incapable of securing social
position and that pecuniary advantage has to be 'converted' into status
gains by being ostentatiously displayed. It is not sufficient merely to
possess wealth or power—they must be put in evidence, for esteem is
awarded only on evidence.

Veblen identified two principal ways in which superiority of ownership and achievement come to be transmitted. Firstly, the wealthier an
individual then the more able he is to adopt an affluent lifestyle dominated by 'conspicuous leisure'.[25] This serves to demonstrate to others
an ability to consume time in non-productive ways and to abstain in
large part from any form of productive work. The status given to those
members of society who can afford not to work has traditionally been
considerable and by the same token many highly productive occupations
are often seen as vulgar and menial and totally incompatible with life

on a satisfactory spiritual or social plane. The need to work comes to be associated in men's thoughts with inferior economic and social status and a person's prestige therefore grows if he can demonstrate—by consuming large amounts of leisure time—that he does not have to work to survive and prosper.

For conspicuous leisure to be effective in securing recognition it has to be consumed in a manner and environment which unequivocally demonstrates the high relative wealth of the consumer and must be complemented by ostentatious and often wasteful consumption. The use of servants, for example, to undertake certain tasks and to wait on the interests and comforts of the individual is clearly a strong indicator of wealth but the maintenance of servants who produce nothing and are entirely 'surplus to requirements' would argue still higher wealth and position. Leisure must therefore be significantly conspicuous only in terms of the wealth and resources it consumes.

In addition to conspicuous leisure, Veblen argued that a second and increasingly more important means of wealth display is available to the status-seeker—that of 'conspicuous consumption'.[26] As with conspicuous leisure, ostentatious expenditure is seen to be motivated not by the direct utility of the 'consumption' in question but by the opportunity it affords for establishing relative financial superiority. The ostentatious display of goods and services which are both expensive and highly valued by others provides the individual with an alternative path to social prestige in any society which recognises wealth as a major determinant of status-conference.

All goods consumed for display purposes normally have to conform to some minimum level of quality but it is the value or cost of the products in question which offers utility to the consumer. Product utility is ultimately determined only by the reaction of other members of the community to the 'price' of the purchase; the higher the price is known (or believed) to be then the greater the recognition given to the accumulated wealth of the buyer.

To be really effective, conspicuous consumption also needs a strong element of 'conspicuous waste'—'waste because this expenditure does not serve human life or human well-being on the whole and not because it is waste or misdirection of effort or expenditure as viewed from the standpoint of the individual consumer who chooses it'.[27] The obvious implication for expenditure on goods and services which is intended to display wealth is that it should be an expenditure of superfluities. In order to be reputable it should be wasteful. The waste element is in fact seen as necessarily very large in conspicuous consumption as this secures the high price of the product in question.

In any society in which the basis of social status is pecuniary strength, therefore, conspicuous leisure and the unproductive consumption of goods are essential marks of prowess and activities necessary to ensure recognition within the community. The utility of both lies in the element of waste which each displays; conspicuous leisure needs to waste time and effort and conspicuous consumption needs to waste money and productive resources. Both 'are methods of demonstrating the possession of wealth and the two are conventionally accepted as equivalents'.[28]

Conspicuous leisure and consumption are in evidence in the earliest societies. However, as societies evolve and the distribution of income and wealth becomes more broadly based, the opportunity for such behaviour is extended to those who in more primitive feudal communities would have neither the right nor the financial resources to behave conspicuously. Veblen saw the link between ostentatious display and wealth as beyond dispute but argued at the same time that once individuals in the later industrialised societies were able to meet their basic primary needs then a proportion of income was given over to status-motivated conspicuous expenditure regardless of the individual's relative income position or social class.[29] He also believed that the relative importance and incidence of conspicuous consumption can and does change as one descends the social and economic scale. In traditional societies, conspicuous leisure is easily affordable by the small elites who control the vast majority of the community's wealth. As these societies develop, however, there are substantial changes in social structure, wealth becomes more equally distributed, the financial and political ability of individuals to choose not to work is progressively reduced and conspicuous consumption gains in relative importance.[30]

Veblen's views were strongly (even exclusively) shaped by his observations of late nineteenth century American society. He believed that the relative attractiveness of conspicuous leisure and conspicuous consumption at that time was determined by the social and economic environment in which the individual found himself. In fact, social trends were clearly beginning to make conspicuous consumption more attractive. Firstly, conspicuous leisure is most effective when the social group in which it is displayed is relatively small and where personal acquaintance is strong, but in America social groups were beginning to be more broadly based and considerably more impersonal. Overt consumption, therefore, began to appear more likely to gain recognition. The new urban society was far more conspicuous in terms of consumption than the earlier rural communities which had been typified by small, highly personalised reference groups. Secondly, the 'modern' society of the nineteenth century created conditions in which geographic neighbours were not social neighbours or even acquaintances but nevertheless their good opinion often seemed of great importance to an individual or household. Conspicuous leisure could gain nothing in the way of added prestige and respect (it could even suggest to observers that the consumer was perhaps unemployed and/or poor and would cause not a gain but a

9

significant reduction in conferred status). The only sure method of communicating relative wealth and securing social recognition in such circumstances was to impress people through an ability to pay for products and services of acknowledged 'quality'—i.e. high price.

In addition to structural changes in society, Veblen believed that the economics of social stratification has its own considerable influence on the balance between conspicuous leisure and consumption. As the social order descends, leisure becomes harder and harder to achieve. There comes a point on the economic scale where the husband must work to support his family and so he passes the responsibility for conspicuous leisure to his wife. Still lower down the scale the wife also is forced to work to supplement the family income and the consumption of leisure tends to disappear.[31] Similarly with conspicuous consumption. If the husband is obliged to forego conspicuous expenditures then the responsibility for maintaining a socially 'decent' level of conspicuous consumption falls on the wife. Overall consumption patterns must reach a required standard, however, because households in each particular social stratum (and this is held to be true for all societies and all levels of development) implicitly recognise an 'expected' standard of living and strive to maintain the standard. This ideal of decency is often based on the lifestyle and standards of the next highest stratum in the social hierarchy but families believe that they risk forfeiting both their status and good name if they do not conform to the accepted code, at least in appearance.[32]

Conspicuous leisure and consumption are therefore seen as desirable objectives in all social groups but it is economics—i.e. the absolute and relative levels of income and wealth—which ultimately decides to what extent they can be undertaken. Conspicuous leisure is greatly reduced or eliminated when both man and wife are obliged to work to maintain the standard of living of the household but, in contrast, conspicuous consumption can and does continue at far lower social and economic levels. The socio-economic depths at which conspicuous consumption is still in evidence have never been established but even at real poverty levels such behaviour has been 'reported' and Veblen himself noted that 'no class of society, not even the most abjectly poor, foregoes all customary conspicuous consumption. The last items of this category of consumption are not given up except under stress of the direst necessity. High levels of squalor and discomfort will be endured before the last pretence of pecuniary decency is abandoned. . . There is no class and no country that has yielded so abjectly before the pressure of physical want as to deny themselves all gratifications of this higher or spiritual need.'[33]

As the individual's economic circumstances change, therefore, the ability to conspicuously consume changes pro rata but the overall motivation so to do is, according to Veblen, undiminished. Such behaviour is seen more as a social need rather than as a relatively superficial consumer preference. However, it is also possible that the objectives of conspicuous consumption may change as the individual's income and wealth changes. When high levels of discretionary income are available, conspicuous behaviour may well be more 'aggressive' in that it seeks to gain recognition for the individual or family from higher socio-economic groups whilst at the same time reinforcing superiority of status over lower groups. As personal financial circumstances deteriorate, however, conspicuous consumption is more likely to be 'defensive' with the intention not of making positive social gains but of securing existing status within current membership groups.

Summarising, Thorstein Veblen argued that individuals within any particular community feel a basic need to secure and improve their status in society. He saw conspicuous consumption as an unavoidable consequence of a pattern of social evolution which gives ever increasing recognition and importance to wealth as the major de facto determinant of social position and prestige. Under such social conditions, the individual needs not only to accumulate the wealth necessary to finance his status aspirations but subsequently needs to display this wealth in order to establish his status claim with society at large or with a specific socio-economic group. Conspicuous consumption proves an ideal vehicle for wealth display and becomes increasingly important—at the expense of conspicuous leisure—as societies become more industrialised and as the distribution of income and wealth becomes more equitable. Furthermore, the greater the element of 'conspicuous waste' in such behaviour then the greater its effectiveness will be.

Veblen believed not only that 'pure' conspicuous consumption serves as a means to status improvement and reinforcement but also that there is often a strong element of ostentatious economic display in other forms of consumer behaviour which on the surface appear to be totally unrelated to consumption motivated by pecuniary emulation and conspicuous waste.[34] As an example, the apparent satisfaction obtained from possessing an article of great 'taste' or beauty may often be no more than a disguise for the real reason for satisfaction—that is, that others will recognise the considerable cost of the product and will consequently come to admire the individual's ability to find the money to purchase it. The ownership and display of diamonds serves as a good illustration; no matter how outstanding the stones are seen to be, the owner's actual utility in possession may well derive for the greater part from audience reaction to the very high price which must have been paid to obtain them. In cases of this type, taste and cost come to be interrelated and expensiveness comes to be accepted as a tasteful feature of the articles in question, being a mark of 'honorific costliness'.

Secondly, it is possible that with many products purchased primarily for their direct utility, the admiration of others for the purchase is often an additional 'spiritual' bonus which may subconsciously have influenced the original decision to buy.[35] There may consequently be a considerable (unrevealed) element of conspicuous consumption in the purchase of socially visible products needed and bought predominantly for direct utility rather than for display.

Following publication of *The Theory of the Leisure Class* at the turn of the century, little immediate attention was given to conspicuous consumption per se. The political and economic implications of such behaviour received more substantial treatment—particularly in the United States in the years up to the First World War—but comment was by and large restricted to condemnation of ostentatious economic display as a social evil and to political prescriptions for its suppression and elimination (q.v.).

Veblen's views on the sociology of conspicuous consumption went largely unchallenged. His diagnosis was quickly accepted as being correct in spite of the fact that it was certainly possible to identify several areas in which his assumptions and conclusions were empirically unfounded or unproven. The wide acceptance of his analysis of socially inspired economic behaviour must have surprised Veblen himself who had defensively conceded in the preface of his book that:

> partly for reasons of convenience, and partly because there is less chance of misapprehending the sense of phenomena that are familiar to all men, the data employed to illustrate or enforce the argument have by preference been drawn from everyday life, by direct observation or through common notoriety, rather than from more recondite sources at a farther remove. It is hoped that no one will find his scientific fitness offended by this recourse to homely facts. . .[36]

Furthermore, he insisted that it was pointless to give detailed reference to those 'articles of theory' on which his premises were based as these were well known and would be 'readily traceable to their source by fairly well-read persons'.

Notwithstanding these admitted shortcomings, no empirical studies were subsequently undertaken to either confirm or refute the sociological foundations of *The Theory of the Leisure Class* and this must be considered surprising in view of the central importance of Veblen's work to many subsequent contributions to sociology and social psychology.

Post-Veblen economic studies of conspicuous consumption were also remarkable only by their absence, economists in general still subscribing to the view put forward by Alfred Marshall that 'the economist studies mental states rather through their manifestations than in themselves'.[37] There was some later dissent from this view. Keynes saw the importance of these 'mental states' by arguing that economists have to recognise that the needs of human beings 'fall into two classes—those needs which are absolute in the sense that we feel them whatever the situation of our fellow human beings may be and those which are relative only in that their satisfaction lifts us above, makes us feel superior to, our fellow'.[38] In his *General Theory*, Keynes devoted a chapter to the subjective factors which together may influence the individual's propensity to consume and included in these factors those of ostentation and extravagance.[39] However, this recognition of the existence and role of ostentatious economic display, coupled with the earlier rebuke to conventional economic wisdom in choosing to ignore such behaviour, did little or nothing to generate a greater general interest in what could be termed the psychology of demand.

In more recent years, several factors have combined to make conspicuous consumption—at least theoretically—a more obviously rewarding area of study. The Keynesian belief that economics can not realistically ignore behavioural influences on demand formation has gained in authority. The development of affluent, mass consumption societies over the last twenty years has provided ample evidence that, contrary to many expectations, conspicuous economic display has neither disappeared nor become irrelevant in consumer eyes but has for the most part been modified and used as an important element in demand management (q.v.). The behavioural aspects of consumption—particularly in relation to socially visible goods—are clearly of some considerable importance in helping to explain how such societies function both socially and economically. There has consequently been an increasing interest in the psychology as well as the economics of the market place and a greater emphasis on the importance of many social influences on consumer preference formation which, on exclusively economic criteria, would appear to be irrational and of little real relevance.

Researchers found it increasingly difficult to attempt comprehensive analyses of modern consumer demand in purely economic terms and have been compelled to attempt some accommodation of the 'irrational' psychological and social elements which have continued to play an important role in determining many demand patterns. A far heavier emphasis has been given to consumer behaviour as opposed to consumption economics in those particular areas of demand which are acknowledged to be motivated primarily by non-economic factors.[40] However, progress has at best been limited. In particular, explanations of the phenomenon of conspicuous consumption remain unsatisfactory and no real advance has been made on the socio-economic 'theories' of Veblen and his predecessors described in this chapter.

The fundamental obstacle to a better understanding of conspicuous consumption has been the lack of theoretical research into the subject in more recent years. Veblen had recognised that knowledge of the basic social and economic conditions which create such behaviour must come before empirical analysis, for without a greater theoretical understanding of the causes of ostentatious display observations of conspicuous consumption must necessarily continue to be 'random' and often inexplicable. The following chapter therefore concentrates on an examination of those factors which together shape social environment and which can be expected to influence the propensity to conspicuously consume.

Notes

1   See Hume, D., *Discourse of Trade*, 1680. There were some who felt that luxury consumption was acceptable provided such expenditures were controlled. Two conditions were usually proposed —firstly, that gold and silver were not used in the manufacture of such goods and secondly, that the use of imported goods was not allowed (Fortrey, S., *England's Interest and Improvement*, 1673, reprinted in McCulloch, J.R. (ed) *Early English Tracts on Commerce*, Cambridge, 1952.

2   See Johnson, E.A., *Predecessors of Adam Smith*, Kelley, New York, 1965, p.290.

3   Dobbs, A., *An Essay on Trade and Improvement of Ireland*, Dublin, 1729, p.52.

4   North, Sir Dudley, *Discourse upon Trade*, Thos. Basset at The George in Fleet Street, London, 1691, pp.14-5. The same theme was also developed by Bernard de Mandeville, *The Grumbling Hive*, (later 'The Fable of the Bees'), 1705.

5   The only exception seemed to be that of a ruler's personal extravagance which was seen to be a necessary reinforcement of his position and office. Aristocrat excesses were therefore treated in a far more sympathetic manner.

6   Locke, J., *Some Considerations of the Consequences of Lowering of Interest and Raising the Value of Money*, 1692.

7   Smith's views on conspicuous economic behaviour are examined in some detail in Riesman, D.A., *Adam Smith's Sociological Economics*, Croom Helm, London, 1976, especially pp.102-17.

8   Smith, A., *Theory of Moral Sentiments*, 1759, p.86. In fact the empirical proof of the effectiveness of wealth in securing social status is simply Smith's claim that 'it almost constantly obtains it'.

9   See Riesman, D.A., op.cit., p.114.

10 Smith, A., *The Wealth of Nations*, vol.1, p.192.

11 How it ensures this power is not made clear. Presumably the conspicuous behaviour of the rich is seen as a reinforcement of existing class structures and privileges and encourages a deference and belief in the status quo amongst the less fortunate.

12 Smith, A., *Theory of Moral Sentiments,* op.cit., p.153.

13 Rae, J., *The Sociological Theory of Capital,* (1834) Macmillan, New York, 1905.

14 Ibid., pp.252, 245-7.

15 Marshall, A., *Principles of Economics,* Macmillan, London, 1890; as reference 8th edition, Macmillan, London, 1964.

16 Ibid., p.73.

17 Ibid., p.113.

18 Veblen, T., *The Theory of the Leisure Class,* first published in New York (Macmillan) 1899; first UK edition, 1925; as reference UK edition, 3rd impression, George Allen and Unwin, London, 1957.

19 Ibid., p.23.

20 Ibid., p.24.

21 Ibid., p.29.

22 Ibid., chapter 2.

23 Ibid., p.31.

24 Ibid., pp.31-2.

25 Ibid., chapter 3.

26 Ibid., chapter 4.

27 Ibid., pp.97-8.

28 Ibid., p.85.

29 Ibid., chapter 5, The Pecuniary Standard of Living.

30 Veblen never saw conspicuous leisure and conspicuous consumption as exclusively 'upper class' in terms of motivation. Rather, he argued that the 'balance' between the two changes as economic opportunity itself changes (q.v.).

31 Veblen, T., op.cit., p.84.

32 Ibid., p.84.

33 Ibid., p.85.

34 Ibid., p.100.

35 This concept of spiritual satisfaction contrasts markedly with the view held by many classical economists, for example, that conspicuous consumption is essentially 'trivial' behaviour.

36 Veblen, T., op.cit., preface.

37 Marshall, A., op.cit., p.16.

38 Keynes, J.M., *Essays in Persuasion, Economic Possibilities for our Grandchildren*, Macmillan, London, 1931, pp.365-6.

39 Keynes, J.M., *General Theory of Employment, Interest and Money*, Macmillan, London, 1936 — chapter 9, The Propensity to Consume: The Subjective Factors.

40 Writers such as Katona, Galbraith and Packard were among the first to recognise the substantial role of social aspirations and expectations in shaping demand for socially visible goods (q.v.).

2 The propensity to conspicuously consume: a theoretical explanation

Two conflicting explanations of conspicuous consumption were identified in the last chapter. The 'traditional' view which pre-dated Adam Smith and which was later restated by Rae and Marshall argued that such behaviour is in essence motivated by exclusively personal considerations and owes little or nothing to the social and economic environment in which men live. In contrast, Smith and Veblen believed that ostentatious economic display is generated by specific socio-economic conditions which make the conspicuous display of wealth a necessary activity for those seeking higher personal status and prestige within the community. Although the so-called 'Veblen Effect' has been widely accepted as the more plausible explanation of such behaviour, the earlier hypothesis merits some further consideration.

Those who believe conspicuous consumption to be socially 'uncontrolled' and motivated solely by self-indulgence and vanity argue by implication if not explicitly that the desire for economic display is randomly decided by innate personality difference between individuals in any given community. Personality differences are in turn seen to be determined by genetic variables which are quite independent of a community's social and economic structure.

This argument can find some theoretical support. Early theories of personality and motivation centred strongly on non-environmental, instinct directed drives—the 'id' and 'ego' of Freudian analysis, the 'collective unconscious' of Jung—which are only modified by social and defensive factors to ensure that individual behaviour does not threaten or undermine the interests of society at large. However, the belief that individual actions are shaped by personality traits which are randomly determined in the individual has been strongly challenged in more recent years by those who take the view that individuals are primarily motivated by social goals which are dominated in the mature individual by the standard of the community in which he lives. A person is accordingly never in an isolated or static situation—any action in the social environment will create a reaction to which he or she must adjust. Whilst accepting that uncontrolled, inherited instincts do influence overall personality, the need to conform socially and the overt or covert striving towards social goals is seen to overwhelm the unconscious instincts and ensure that behaviour is dominated by social considerations.[1]

The society oriented concept of personality development clearly challenges the assumptions made by those who believed conspicuous consumption to be an uncomplicated consequence of self-indulgence and vanity. Modern psychoanalysts have tended to favour the view that personality develops and redevelops over an individual's lifespan according to the social influences to which he is exposed. However, even if the general case for social conditioning of personality is conceded, it may still be argued that the particular phenomenon of conspicuous consumption is motivated by exceptional factors which remain independent of social and economic environment. Notwithstanding the process of socialisation, vanity and self-indulgence may be seen as unlearned drives which are not socially 'conditioned' by environment and will always be in evidence regardless of a community's social and economic structure. To what extent can such an interpretation of conspicuous consumption motives be justified?

Motivation theory has long recognised the proposition that human needs fall into two general categories. Primary (biogenic) needs are essentially physiological and cover such bodily functions as hunger, thirst, sex, sleep and exercise. Individuals have no choice but to meet such needs—at least to some minimum level—if they wish to survive, and the motivation to satisfy these basic drives is therefore innate and unlearned. These fundamental needs are for the most part unconscious, uncontrollable and non-environmental and can be seen to represent the motives of the Freudian 'id' and a part of Jung's 'collective unconscious'. Secondary (psychogenic) needs, in contrast, comprise a more sophisticated structure of psychological needs which clearly relate to social, cultural and intellectual interests. Unlike primary drive, secondary motives are essentially emotional, social and psychological in nature and are not necessary (directly at least) to physical survival.

Individuals may tolerate partial satisfaction of both primary and secondary needs but the level of satisfaction demanded will always be greater for the life-supporting primary wants. Minimal physiological and safety needs will therefore always take precedence over higher order (social) wants although it is generally accepted that some individuals may direct their attention to social motives which come to dominate actions and behaviour even when lower needs remain urgent.[2]

Looking at conspicuous consumption with particular reference to this 'hierarchy of needs', apologists for the traditional explanation of ostentatious economic display need to establish that vanity is, in essence, a primary rather than a secondary drive and that it is a personality trait which owes little or nothing to social influences or pressures. However, this argument would appear difficult to support. If the dominant drive behind economic display is independent of social conditioning then the consumer is seeking to reassure only himself and so has no need to make his consumption conspicuous to others. If self-satisfaction is the basic motive then the need to make purchases and consumption socially visible does not exist and the display element is both unnecessary and irrelevant. However, conspicuous consumption is by definition a form of consumer behaviour in which third-party opinion of the transaction and the consumption is the principal source of satisfaction for the individual consumer.

An alternative defence of the traditional view is possible, that conspicuous consumption is a form of vanity or indulgence aimed at a particular social 'audience' but that the basic drive is unlearned and would be significant under any social conditions. Veblen himself often referred to conspicuous consumption as a 'spiritual' need and seemed at times to be suggesting that such behaviour, although socially inspired, could be instinctive and innate. But again it is difficult to believe that any form of behaviour which requires the participation of other members of a particular social group (and this is true of conspicuous consumption, which needs an audience if it is to succeed) is generated directly and exclusively within the individual rather than as a result of his social experiences and interpersonal relationships within the community.

The belief that ostentatious economic display is a function of primary rather than of secondary or psychological drives is therefore not easily supported. Certainly some few conspicuous consumers may take a simple, vicarious pleasure only in the self-indulgence of such consumption and may feel, as Rae argued, that economic waste is a sufficient reward in itself but the balance of probability based on observation and report suggests that most luxury or ostentatious consumption which is meant to impress other people and which relies for its effect on the response of third parties to a particular purchase or act of consumption. However, in rejecting the argument that overall levels of conspicuous consumption are randomly determined by certain personality traits which encourage the use of wealth-display as an expression of personal vanity, it would be a mistake to believe that personality differences play no role in determining a particular individual's propensity to conspicuously consume. The influence of personality variables on such behaviour will be considered later in this section.

If the traditional explanation of conspicuous consumption motives is not acceptable, an alternative hypothesis is needed. Both Smith and Veblen were unhappy with the view that such behaviour is an innate, unlearned response and argued that, far from being determined by independent personality traits, the incidence of conspicuous economic display is decided by social and economic environment. The propensity to conspicuously consume is therefore seen to be decided by the values and norms of the societies in which men live. A combination of favourable social circumstances will provide the impetus for conspicuous consumption and will motivate many individuals to adopt this exceptional form of consumer behaviour without fear of social condemnation. Conversely, the environment within a particular community may be so hostile to such behaviour that the majority of consumers will reject the possibility of seeking to establish social standing and prestige through the use of conspicuous consumption and will adopt other means to the same end.

This view of ostentatious display (the 'Veblen Effect') has been widely accepted as offering the most plausible explanation of observed conspicuous consumption and is certainly supported by more recent evidence relating to the effects of social and economic environment on individual attitudes in general and on consumer behaviour in particular. In accepting the Veblen hypothesis as the basis for further research, however, it is first of all necessary to identify and examine those socio-economic factors to which Veblen indirectly refers and which may be considered of prime importance in determining the 'climate' in which social and economic consumption takes place.

Perhaps the greatest single influence we can expect on individual and group consumer behaviour comes from a community's cultural values.[3] Such values will naturally vary from society to society and there can be striking differences in outlook between societies at different points of social and economic evolution. Traditional communities for example tend to look at the past in that each generation is expected to learn its roles from its fathers and to regard them as the only teachers and examplars. Such societies are therefore seen to be intellectually self-sufficient and any behaviour which seems to reject or challenge the values which have been passed on from generation to generation is roundly condemned and repressed. In contrast, more developed societies look to the present and the future; norms of the past can be legitimately questioned and there tends to be a far higher degree of social economic and intellectual freedom.

An individual learns the values of his culture through the process of socialisation and can not avoid the cultural biases inherent in the groups and institutions which transmit these values to him. In addition to exposure to a general culture, he will react to sub-cultures to which he belongs or relates and which can have a significant influence on his beliefs and lifestyle. Sub-cultures, normally identified on the basis of nationality, religion, race or geography, strive to maintain their separate existence by ensuring that individuals introduced into the group are taught and encouraged to amend broader cultural values and belief systems in order to better conform to the sub-culture's norms.

The overall cultural system of a society at any point in time will be composed of a variety of sub-systems and every member of that society will have a place in several of these sub-systems. Each individual belongs to a particular age-sex, ethnic or religious group and so forth. These component parts do not stand separately from the total culture but complement the system and, by and large, share its fundamental and dominant values. The overlapping influences of sub-cultures on the behaviour of individuals must therefore be recognised, as must the fact that there are many values among sub-groups within the overall structure.[4]

Cultural and sub-cultural norms will be transmitted to the individual primarily by the family—an entity which to some observers often comprises a sub-culture in its own right. The family role in transmitting these values is of great significance; the influence of the family on its members is pervasive in that the individual in his formative years is constantly exposed to family attitudes, interests, prejudices and motivations which are likely to be a major influence on his actions throughout his adult life. The extent to which he will subsequently abide by values learned in childhood and not seek to question or reject them is, however, determined by the attitudes and structure of the wider 'family' within which the family is itself contained.[5]

The general culture and specific sub-cultures to which an individual is exposed and to whose behavioural norms he consciously or subconsciously subscribes can be expected to have a profound effect on his overall propensity to conspicuously consume. For conspicuous consumption to be worthwhile, ostentatious behaviour in consumption must be recognised as acceptable behaviour by the dominant culture groups within the society. Many traditional societies, for example, treat any overt display of material (or financial) superiority as something to be condemned. There are also communities which reject the concept of competition between men and, in doing so, implicitly reject what is seen to be competitive 'posing' and 'superior' economic behaviour.[6] Many religious sub-cultures strongly oppose the overt display of wealth and would certainly be quick to reject any suggestion that a superiority of displayed riches forms a legitimate basis for added status and prestige.[7] In contrast, there are societies and cultures which actively encourage conspicuous consumption as an illustration to observers—both inside and outside the community—of the rewards given to those who have adopted the particular norms and values of the society as a whole.

Conspicuous consumption should be most acceptable—and should therefore be most in evidence—in those societies whose cultural mores allow and possibly promote the display of pecuniary and material advantage. A nation's culture at any point in time will be determined by the particular sub-cultures which are predominant and which therefore have the greatest influence on overall cultural values. At the national level, approval of conspicuous consumption will depend in large part on whether such behaviour enjoys consensus approval of the dominant sub-cultures but it is important to recognise that strong approval of ostentatious economic display could exist in specific non-dominant sub-cultures at the same time as there is a general public reaction against such behaviour as being anti-social and unacceptable. Consequently, it should theoretically be possible to observe high levels of conspicuous consumption undertaken by certain individuals within societies whose overall 'national' culture implicitly or explicitly rejects such behaviour.

A second major influence on the nature and incidence of conspicuous consumption can be expected to derive from social class structure and differences in class membership. In any stratified society, class necessarily directs human activity—indeed, social class is itself often categorised, with much justification, as a specific sub-culture in its own right. In more modern societies there is today some debate as to whether class distinctions still retain their traditional importance, but even if it may no longer dominate behaviour it must still be considered a highly significant influence on social and consumer behaviour.[8]

In any society which seeks to function efficiently social order is endemic and seems to evolve naturally as people in a community come to accept various responsibilities and realise that it is impossible to avoid a degree of social stratification if progress is to be made and a minimum level of social and economic order maintained. Although such stratification is common to most if not all societies, one point of difference tends to be the criteria on which people are judged to be socially distinct and separate from each other. In traditional communities, distinctions are commonly made on the basis of variables over which the individual has little or no control—i.e. age, sex, inheritance, family connection, etc. Social stratification in the Indian caste system, for example, is definite, institutionalised and offers the individual no control over his social grading—a grading which will stay with him for life and which is based primarily on the past occupational or sectarian activities of his family or village. In contrast, many modern societies allow a far greater level of social mobility and it is easier for a person to move from class to class on the basis of controllable factors such as education, current occupation or achieved wealth. The type of society to which an individual belongs, therefore, will tend to determine his social class and also the extent to which he will be allowed to 'move' from class to class over his lifetime or seek to secure a higher class ranking for his children.

In considering the relationship between social class and conspicuous consumption it is tempting to believe that such behaviour would be restricted for predominantly financial reasons to the upper classes or elites of a particular society. However, this interpretation is too simplistic. Veblen—arguing politically as well as academically—identified conspicuous expenditure as being not only highly significant in the behaviour patterns of the upper classes but also a phenomenon which extends to all levels of society and to all social classes. If conspicuous consumption does occur in all social classes, however, what will certainly differ according to social class membership will be the type and level of conspicuous consumption that takes place. Certain social classes will accept conspicuous display as a legitimate activity more than others and it seems probable that ostentatious financial behaviour will enjoy greater recognition in those classes which accept income or wealth as the major determinant of social status both within and without the group. If conspicuous consumption is approved by an individual's own social class but is condemned by high class groups, then 'horizontally-directed' conspicuous expenditure can be expected—that is, conspicuous behaviour intended to maintain existing social status within a particular social class or, perhaps more ambitiously, seeking to achieve preferential or superior status within the group. In contrast, if all social classes are prepared to accept the conspicuous display of wealth for ranking purposes then individuals may channel their expenditure into achieving 'vertical' status gains by securing recognition and prestige from higher class groups in order to make positive between-group social advances.

The aspect of social class structure which will have the most marked effect on the nature and level of ostentatious consumption is therefore the degree of social mobility that is allowed by any particular national or cultural group and the extent to which revealed wealth can secure such mobility. In socially rigid societies where little or no mobility is allowed between social groups, conspicuous consumption will achieve nothing if it attempts to break down traditional barriers based on occupation, birth or family. The incentive to spend conspicuously to achieve vertical status gains would therefore be insignificant. However, status gains within a particular class or 'caste' would certainly be possible and a considerable level of 'horizontal' conspicuous consumption could be expected. In those other societies which encourage a far greater level of social mobility and in which wealth is clearly recognised as a means of social advancement, 'vertical' status gains are more easily achieved and between-group conspicuous economic display should therefore be far more in evidence.

The greater the recognition of wealth as a social class determinant, therefore, the greater the incentive to behave conspicuously and to display such wealth either for horizontal or vertical gains. There would seem to be little doubt that social class has been increasingly decided by wealth as societies have evolved. At the same time, there is reason to believe that the sensitivity of individuals to social class rankings has noticeably diminished in the more modern affluent societies and this may well have served to depress the level not of conspicuous consumption per se but of consumption specifically undertaken and intended to secure status gains measured in traditional class terms.

People naturally tend to form close friendships and relationships with those of equal social status and also subscribe to the views and attitudes which membership of a particular class implies. In addition to social class, however, modern societies in particular have seen the development and growing importance of many other interactive social groupings which can have a significant influence on the behaviour and aspirations of individual members of a society.[9]

Two principal categories of social groupings can be identified which both play an important part in shaping an individual's lifestyle and behaviour. Firstly, membership groups comprise those associations of people to which a person necessarily or voluntarily belongs and which impose a set of norms regarding the behaviour of members. Such groups may be formal, with defined organisational structures and clearly specified rights and duties, or informal associations in which codes of behaviour are loosely defined and voluntarily adhered to. Both types of group, however, will expect individual membership to be unequivocal and committed. In contrast, aspirant groups are those to which the individual may wish to belong but of which he is currently not a member. The motivations and ambitions of each member of the community will in large part determine the non-membership groups to which he or she will aspire and a significant part of their social and economic behaviour will inevitably reflect a concern to gain the recognition of such groups.

Membership and aspirant groups taken together form what is recognised as a person's 'reference groups'—that is they comprise the groups with which an individual closely identifies himself and so become the standards of evaluation and the sources of his personal behaviour norms. The individual seeks firstly to maintain membership of groups which recognise him as a member and secondly seeks to attain membership of those groups to which he 'refers' but of which he is not a member. There would seem little doubt that these reference groups do play a role of major significance in deciding the actions and reactions of human beings to the stimuli to which they are exposed and greatly affect individual behaviour patterns.

In so far as reference groups are concerned, conspicuous consumption will be motivated not by social class distinctions but by how effective such consumption is seen to be in gaining the approval or membership of aspirant groups to which the individual refers. Reference groups often have clearly defined conventions with regards to patterns of personal expenditure and consumption and members—both actual and potential—will be expected to conform to such norms.

The groups which are most likely to actively encourage acts of conspicuous consumption are logically those who see the possession and display of wealth either as a prerequisite of group membership or as something which confers added prestige within a particular group. However, the fact that most people relate to multiple reference groups and are sensitive to the influences of many separate sources makes the situation far more complicated than it at first appears. Multiple group membership and aspiration—whether familial, occupational, political, educational or economic—creates the possibility of conflict in that consumption behaviour which is 'approved' by some groups may be totally unacceptable to others. Normally a person will attempt to resolve such conflicts by occupying the behavioural middle ground in an attempt to offend no group to extreme; but often such an option is unrealistic and the problem remains. Unlike the conditions which prevail for many other forms of social behaviour, conspicuous consumption by definition cannot easily be concealed from one group whilst at the same time being deliberately revealed to another. Consequently, a choice is forced on the individual which must necessarily offend one or other of such reference groups.[10]

It would seem reasonable to argue that pressures both for and against conspicuous consumer behaviour will build up for individuals responding to multiple reference groups. The strength of a person's motivation to conspicuously consume—in so far as reference group influences are concerned—will be directly related to the 'mix' of the groups of which he is a member or to which he aspires, and secondly to any rank order of preference between groups which the individual is forced to make. If all groups condone and reward conspicuous consumption then the incidence of such behaviour will, other things being equal, be high. If a proportion of the groups reward such behaviour and these groups rank high on the individual's preference scale of membership and aspirant groups, then again conspicuous economic behaviour should be much in evidence. Conversely, if groups rejecting such behaviour appear most important to the would-be consumer, then little or no conspicuous expenditure would be expected or undertaken.

As with social class, conspicuous consumption directed at reference groups will have either horizontal (within-group) or vertical (between-group) objectives. Display behaviour directed at existing membership groups will be primarily horizontal although there may be a vertical element in such expenditure if there is a desire to establish a clear position of opinion leadership within the group. Consumption intended to secure recognition of aspirant groups may be either horizontal or vertical depending on the financial or material status of the target group.

Three variables have been considered as major environmental determinants of the level and direction of conspicuous consumption in any given society. At the same time it has been shown that the potential for conflict is present in all three. General cultural values may be in direct conflict with the particular sub-cultures to which an individual responds; conspicuous behaviour may be acceptable within certain social classes but rejected by others; finally, the value systems of two or more reference groups may be irreconcilable. The individual in any community is therefore faced with the problem of needing to conform to the expectations and norms of his cultural and social membership groups whilst at the same time seeking to achieve recognition from other (aspirant) groups through which he may hope to establish status gains. In the final analysis, behaviour with respect to conspicuous consumption will be determined by his order of priorities and by the strength of existing group affinities.

Both Smith and Veblen analysed conspicuous consumption in general rather than in specific terms and consequently offered a general theory to explain the phenomenon. However, whilst culture, social class and reference group influences may provide an acceptable explanation of aggregate attitude formation and consumer behaviour in so far as economic display is concerned, they fail to offer an explanation as to why attitudes with respect to conspicuous consumption can vary significantly amongst individuals who are subject to identical or very similar environmental conditioning. It is evident that not all individuals in a particular community share the same views of conspicuous consumption nor are they equally likely to adopt this exceptional pattern of consumer behaviour. Given a near identical social environment, why should such differences occur?

One possible explanation has already been touched upon in part. Earlier in this section the 'traditional' view of conspicuous consumption as being an expression only of vanity or self-indulgence was examined and largely rejected in favour of the 'social conditioning' hypothesis put forward by Veblen. At the same time it was argued that the general importance of individual personality differences could not be totally discounted as a significant influence on purchasing and consumption behaviour. Research into variations of all forms of consumer behaviour suggests that uncontrolled personality factors may be of considerable importance in deciding events. Consequently, whilst the social theory of conspicuous consumption may be acceptable as a general statement— that is as an aggregate theory—it has considerable limitations if it is used to explain or predict the behaviour or attitudes of one particular person with respect to ostentatious display.

It is well established that uncontrolled personality traits can vary significantly between individuals and that these can and do determine peoples' general behaviour patterns to some extent.[11] Whilst accepting the society oriented concept of personality development, it is also true that the ranking and priority given to primary and secondary needs will vary from person to person. The extent to which status, prestige and recognition are considered important will be determined in part by personality differences between individuals who may have shared identical social and economic conditioning processes.

There is no doubt that even people exposed to the same socio-economic environment often display markedly different patterns of social and economic behaviour within the boundaries of what is deemed to be 'acceptable conduct' by the group or community. These behavioural differences may be determined in large part by variations in individual personality traits. Variations can occur in role dispositions relating to individual characteristics such as independence, initiative and dominance; in sociometric dispositions concerning relationships with other people and covering such traits as friendliness and sociability; and in expressive dispositions relating to self-expression and concerned with an individual's level of exhibitionism, , competitiveness, aggression and social poise.[12] Personality 'types' have similarly been identified. Compliant individuals are seen to be relatively insecure and need the closeness, affection and support of others. Aggressive persons seek dominance and feel a need to 'win' or excel both in their public and their private lives. Finally, detached individuals tend to be introspective and private, wish to opt out of competitive society and spend little time in building relationships with others.[13]

Other things (i.e.social environment) being equal, the typical conspicuous consumer should be identifiable as an individual whose dominant personality traits make such behaviour appear to be positive, rewarding or perhaps even necessary. At the same time it is not possible to describe a particular 'set' of personality traits which could be used to identify the conspicuous consumers in any particular group. Conspicuous consumption could, for instance, be attractive both to the aggressive personality type, who would see such behaviour as a means of stimulating social competition, and to the compliant individual seeking to establish or consolidate social group membership. Nevertheless, differences in personality traits can be considered a partial but significant explanation of observed differences in individual propensities to conspicuously consume.

We can reasonably expect individual personality to play some role in determining attitudes to economic display. Social environment and innate personality characteristics may, for example, be in conflict and so reduce levels of conspicuous consumption. Conversely, they may both be 'positive' and ensure that a particular person is highly motivated to conspicuously consume. However, whilst recognising the relevance of personality differences, there is a far more fundamental explanation of individual variations in conspicuous expenditure which may occur within any particular society or social group—an explanation which derives not from the sociology but from the economics of consumption.

Social environment and individual personality provide the motivation to conspicuously consume. Nevertheless, motivation is a necessary but not a sufficient element in deciding whether conspicuous consumption does occur; the desire to display wealth must be complemented by the economic opportunity so to behave. The individual committed to gaining recognition and status through conspicuous consumption is inevitably constrained to a greater or lesser extent by his absolute and relative economic power measured in terms of capital stock, current income and credit status. In short, conspicuous economic display requires not only that a positive motivation exists for the potential consumer but also that he has the necessary financial resources to adopt such a purchasing and consumption policy.

The economics of conspicuous consumption are in reality far more complicated than may appear to be the case at first sight. In essence the ability of any person to consume for display will be directly related to the basic level of discretionary wealth which he commands—that is the wealth remaining after all 'primary' living costs have been met. However, the critical factor in determining the relative attractiveness of display consumption is not only absolute wealth but also discretionary wealth relative to other members of the cultural, socio-economic or membership groups to which an individual refers. As the satisfaction associated with conspicuous consumption is derived from the response of others, this response will be significant only when there is sufficient audience 'respect' for a particular act of conspicuous expenditure and admiration for the cost of such ostentatious behaviour. It is therefore income and wealth relativities and not absolute levels of wealth which we can expect to be the determining factors in encouraging conspicuous consumption.

The conspicuous consumer may have two principal objectives in mind when committing himself to a particular act of display. Firstly, he may be seeking to secure horizontal status gains from others in his existing membership groups or in parallel aspirant groups. Secondly, he may be seeking recognition from higher groups that he should be classified as an equal in terms of social position and prestige. Taking the first case, the decision to purchase or consume a particular good or service will depend on how exceptional the purchase or consumption will be seen to be by fellow group members. If the price paid would normally be considered beyond the purchasing capabilities of the group— or at least would be seen to be a purchase option available only to those group members enjoying above average discretionary buying power—then such a purchase will seem worthwhile to the conspicuous consumer. However, the consumption decision is in practice not an easy one to take as the level of discretionary income enjoyed within any social or socio-economic grouping may vary quite considerably. There may be those within the group who for various reasons have an exceptionally high level of financial obligation which puts them at a clear disadvantage to others who enjoy greater discretionary income. Such group members may well be more readily impressed by acts of conspicuous expenditure or consumption which they themselves could not hope to achieve. In contrast, those enjoying greater levels of discretion with respect to disposal of their income or wealth may find the same acts of display to be singularly unimpressive.

Whilst an individual's absolute level of wealth is largely determined by the social and economic system in which he lives, levels of discretionary income can be and are controlled in part by the individual himself. Discretionary funds are normally considered to be those monies available after all necessary financial and material obligations have been met but people have the choice as to how this minimum level of need and obligation is decided. A standard of living which is regarded as subsistence by one person could be regarded as luxurious by another member of the same social group. Furthermore, there is evidence to suggest that, even at levels generally recognised as subsistence, individuals are often prepared to lower the threshold of their primary needs still further in order to secure discretionary funds for conspicuous status seeking expenditure. In such circumstances it is meaningless to attempt to measure discretionary income in terms of an economic surplus over and above basic subsistence income. It also becomes difficult for the potential conspicuous consumer to gauge how effective a proposed expenditure or purchase is likely to be in gaining the recognition and approval of others in his membership groups.

When conspicuous consumption is motivated by the desire to gain recognition and acceptance from 'higher' (i.e. wealthier) socio-economic groups then the income constraint on the would-be purchaser is even more serious. To be successful, consumption needs to reflect a level of income or wealth which may well be in excess of that normally associated with the individual's existing social or economic group. Under such conditions purchase for display will only succeed if it is able to cross the often considerable economic divide between membership and aspirant groups. As in the case with expenditure or consumption carried out to impress members of one's own group, however, members of higher groups will themselves enjoy differing levels of discretionary income. The conspicuous consumer is once again faced with the problem of impressing individuals who, because of their differing 'net' income situations, may bring significantly different financial criteria to bear on any observed purchase.

In addition to the problems of discretionary wealth differences, a further factor may complicate matters. The objective of the consumer seeking to establish status and prestige either within his own group or with a higher group will only be realised if he can achieve a consensus that his consumption behaviour is both impressive and acceptable. In certain groups such a reaction can only be achieved if dominant opinion leaders can be so persuaded and in many communities group opinion leaders on status evaluation may well be those enjoying the highest levels of discretionary buying power or net income. This makes conspicuous consumption objectives more difficult to achieve in that the display of wealth has to be big enough not only to impress those members of the target audience at or below the wealth or income 'norm' of the group but also those individuals whose wealth is above the norm and whose opinions are deferred to by other group members.

The overall desire and opportunity for significant conspicuous consumption will therefore be determined in economic terms by absolute and relative wealth distribution within any particular society or social grouping. The more unequal the distribution then the fewer the numbers who will have a sufficient economic surplus to invest in ostentatious display and conspicuous waste. However, those few individuals should be capable of particularly high levels of conspicuous consumption. Conversely, societies in which income and wealth are broadly distributed offer a far wider opportunity for such behaviour but do not allow individuals the discretionary conspicuous expenditure opportunities enjoyed by the privileged few in more 'unequal' societies.

Finally, within overall distributions of income and wealth, levels of conspicuous consumption will be influenced by distributions within each specific sub-culture, social class or peer grouping. Again the greater the inequalities of distribution then the fewer the number of people who will be able to gain a conspicuous advantage over their social competitors but the higher the level of individual spending within the group; conversely, the more equal the spread of financial resources then the greater the numbers enjoying some discretionary income at a particular social level but the lower the expected per capita spending on consumption.

The above analysis has argued that conspicuous consumption is in essence created and encouraged by various forms of social and economic stratification. Whilst differing theoretical perspectives have over the years been proposed to explain the nature of such stratification, there is no doubt that it is a significant characteristic of the great majority of societies both traditional and modern.

The prerequisite of any system of stratification is that clear inequalities exist (or are capable of being 'manufactured') between the individual members of a society. Of the major theories put forward to explain how and why communities come to be stratified,[14] three particular sources of inequality are repeatedly stressed. Firstly, there may exist a clearly defined economic stratification which has been seen as the primary cause of class differences and class consciousness. Large income and wealth disparities mean that opportunities will exist for some individuals to express a 'superiority of riches' if they feel motivated to do so.[15] Secondly, stratification may be based on inequalities of power, whether political or occupational. Leadership groups can have very great societal impact and can enjoy a particular advantage over other members of their community. This hierarchical privilege belongs to what has been described as a 'strategic elite' and, as would be expected, there is often a strong link between political and economic power.[16] Finally, there are inequalities based primarily on status differences between individuals where status reflects a widely accepted order of position and social prestige. These status differences may be measured in a number of ways and the criteria used often differ from society to society.[17]

Conspicuous consumption should be a particularly significant factor in those societies which are heavily stratified, particularly in terms of status, and which provide both the motivation and the opportunity for such behaviour. Motivation requires that individuals recognise status as an important element in their lives and lifestyles and believe conspicuous consumption to be a legitimate means of securing status gains or of consolidating existing status levels. This in turn requires a broad cultural, social and economic environment which encourages conspicuous economic display and which has a reward system which confers social prestige on the possession and display of economic superiority. In contrast, the opportunity for conspicuous consumption should be determined by the degree to which inequalities in absolute wealth or in relative discretionary income and wealth levels exist and so allow individuals to differentiate between themselves on the basis of significant variations in economic power.

An attempt has been made in this chapter to identify those social and economic factors which together produce conditions favourable or hostile to conspicuous consumption activity. This is important in that it helps isolate a set of variables which may help to explain instances of conspicuous economic display; however, any theoretical treatment needs to be complemented by a more empirical investigation into patterns of observed conspicuous consumption. Before attempting such a study a framework of enquiry needs to be developed which allows the widest possible analysis of such behaviour but within a clearly structured and productive frame of reference. The following chapter addresses itself to this problem.

Notes

1   The society oriented concept of personality development is most closely associated with the work of Alfred Adler—see, for example,

Adler, A., *Understanding Human Nature,* Greenberg, New York, 1927. His theoretical work has been further developed—see Sullivan, H.S., *The Interpersonal Theory of Psychiatry,* W. Norton, New York, 1953; also Horney, K., *Our Inner Conflicts,* W. Norton, New York, 1945.

2   Maslow, A.H., *Motivation and Personality,* Harper and Row, New York, 1954.

3   A comprehensive literature now exists on the structure and influence of culture on individual personality and behaviour. Reference in this work has been made to: K. Roeber, A.L. and Kluckholm, C., *Culture: A Critical Review of Concepts and Definitions,* Random House, 1963; Tylor, E.B., *Primitive Culture,* 3rd edition, John Murray, London, 1891; Dewey, J., *Democracy and Education,* Macmillan, New York, 1916; Linton, R., *The Cultural Background of Personality,* Appleton-Century, New York, 1945; Banton, M., *An Introduction to the Study of Social Relations,* Tavistock, London, 1968.

4   Arnold, D.O., *The Sociology of Subcultures,* Glendasary Press, Berkeley, California, 1970.

5   See especially, Horney, K., *Our Inner Conflicts,* W. Norton, New York, 1945. Two interesting studies which illustrate the importance of family relationships in transmitting cultural values are: Young, M. and Willmott, P., *Family and Kinship in East London,* Penguin, London, 1957 and Bott, E., *Family and Social Network: Roles Norms and External Relationships in Ordinary Urban Families,* Tavistock, London, 1957.

6   Competition between individuals was, for example, condemned by many North American Indian cultures and the philosophy of 'winning' or 'coming first' in sport or hunting is alien to many other traditional communities throughout the world.

7   See Weber's classic study, *The Protestant Ethnic and the Spirit of Capitalism,* first published in the UK by George Allen and Unwin, 1930.

8   See, inter alia, Warner, W.L., Meeker, M. and Eells, K., *Social Class in America,* Harper and Row, New York, 1960; Sampson, A., *The New Anatomy of Britain,* Hodder and Stoughton, London, 1971; Centers, S., *The Psychology of Social Classes,* Princeton, 1949; Shanks, M., *The Stagnant Society,* Penguin, London, 1972. For commentary, Packard, V., *The Status Seekers,* Penguin, 1969. A good general reference is Thouless, R.H., *General and Social Psychology,* University Tutorial Press, London, 1967.

9 Merton, R.K., *Social Theory and Social Structure,* Free Press, New York, 1957; Hyman, H.H., *The Psychology of Status,* Archives of Psychology, no.269, 1952; Thouless, R.H., op.cit; Asch, S.E., *Social Psychology,* Prentice-Hall, Englewood Cliffs, 1965; Thibaut, J.W. and Kelly, H.H., *The Social Psychology of Groups,* John Wiley and Sons, New York, 1959.

10 Individual personality differences may be of great importance in these circumstances in influencing the final decision on acceptable levels of conspicuous consumption.

11 Some caution is, however, necessary. The hard evidence in favour of innate personality variables being important in consumer decision making is not totally convincing and often lacks measurement and statistical credibility. There is also a substantial amount of contradictory work which has shown no proven relationship between personality and product preference. Nearly all researchers into the subject have been unhappy, to differing extents, about research methodology and the legitimacy of their findings. Kassarjian, in his review of research ('Personality and Consumer Behaviour', *Journal of Marketing Research,* 3 November 1971) concluded: 'the review of studies and papers can be summarized in a single word, equivocal. A few studies indicate a strong relationship between personality and aspects of consumer behaviour, a few indicate no relationship and the great majority indicate that if correlations do exist they are so weak as to be questionable or perhaps meaningless.' Kassarjian identified the questionable validity of personality measuring instruments and was also concerned about the conditions under which most personality tests are held. However, he still supported the view that personality is a significant factor in determining individual consumer behaviour.

12 Krech, D., Crutchfield, R.S. and Ballackey, E.L., *Individual in Society,* McGraw-Hill, New York, 1962.

13 Horney, K., op.cit. Relevant empirical support for Horney's classification of personality types has come from Cohen, J.B., 'An Interpersonal Orientation to the Study of Consumer Behaviour', *Journal of Marketing Research,* 14 August 1967, pp.270-8.

14 Marx, Weber, Pareto and the Functionalists.

15 See Bottomore, T.B. and Rubel, M. (eds), *Karl Marx: Selected Writings,* Penguin, 1963. Also, Titmuss, R.M., *Income Distribution and Social Change,* Allen and Unwin, 1962, and Runciman, W.G., *Relative Deprivation and Social Justice,* Routledge, 1966.

16 Weber, M., *Theory of Social and Economic Organisation,* Free Press, New York; Mills, C. Wright, *The Power Elite,* Oxford

University Press, 1959; Finer, S.E. (ed) *Pareto: Sociological Writings,* Pall Mall Press, 1966; Bottomore, T.B., *Elites and Society,* Penguin, 1966. The concept of the strategic elite is developed in Keller, S., *Beyond the Ruling Class,* Random House, 1963. See also, Mayer, K.B., *Class and Society,* Random House, 1955.

17 See Jackson, J.A. (ed) *Social Stratification,* Cambridge University Press, 1968 and Hatt, P.K., North, C.C. et al., *Occupations and Social Status,* Free Press, New York, 1961. Also Warner, W. Lloyd, Meeker, M. and Eells, K., *Social Class in America,* Harper and Row, Chicago, 1949; Warner, W. Lloyd and Lunt, P.S., *The Social Life of a Modern Community,* Yale University Press, 1941.

The interrelationships of economic power and status inequalities are reviewed in Rex, J., *Key Problems of Sociological Theory,* Routledge, 1951; Giddens, A., *Capitalism and Modern Social Theory,* Cambridge University Press, 1971; Lenski, G.E., *Power and Privilege,* McGraw-Hill, 1966. Also a short discussion in Kelsall, R.K. and Kelsall, H.M., *Stratification,* Longman, London, 1974.

3   Establishing a framework of enquiry

Conspicuous consumption is intended for the most part either to consolidate and secure existing community or group status or to make new 'vertical' status gains within society. It can be seen as a response to particular cultural and social conditions which, together or separately, encourage (or at least do not overtly condemn) the ostentatious display of wealth as a legitimate form of status seeking. This social motivation to conspicuously consume may then be reinforced or diminished by individual personality characteristics which could be strong enough to dominate consumption decisions. Finally, individual opportunity to display will be decided by personal income and wealth measured in both absolute and relative terms.

If this interpretation is correct, it follows that the aggregate level and direction of conspicuous consumption in any society will be primarily determined by the extent to which that society is stratified both socially and economically. Conspicuous economic display should theoretically be most in evidence in societies of unequals and more particularly in those societies which clearly differentiate between individuals at all social levels on the basis of wealth. However, the existence of economic inequalities should only generate conspicuous economic behaviour if the status system specifically recognises the display of wealth as a way to status consolidation and improvement. In societies where wealth and social status are largely unrelated (in many traditional 'caste' systems, for example) then the motivation to conspicuously consume should be considerably reduced or eliminated even though pronounced differences in economic status may exist between individuals.

In moving from theoretical analysis to the problems of research design, this central relationship between social and economic stratification and overall propensities to conspicuously consume must still be recognised. Any suitable framework of reference for research has not only to identify conspicuous consumption in its various forms but must also allow patterns of consumption to be placed within the social and economic contexts in which they occur. Ostentatious economic behaviour is explained only by reference to the particular social conditions which create it and only when instances of conspicuous consumption can be 'matched' to specific socio-economic structures will a comprehensive pattern begin to emerge. It is therefore necessary to 'cluster' observed display consumption to see what significant differences in the level and patterns of such behaviour may exist between different social and economic systems. This objective can itself only be achieved if a relationship between social environment and social character can be established; if different character 'types' linked to specific cultural, social and economic conditions can be identified, and if these types can in turn be associated with particular patterns of conspicuous consumption.

The task of creating an appropriate framework of reference is made easier by past research which has succeeded in isolating three quite fundamental forms of socio-cultural and economic organisation. Firstly, in looking at curves of population growth and distribution it is possible to identify a particular S-shaped curve that appears in the history of the industrialised countries as well as in the projected populations of certain other countries as they are expected to develop in the future. This S-shaped curve starts at a point where the numbers of births and deaths are fairly equal (both birth and death rates being high) and moves through a stage of rapid population increases to a new plateau where births and deaths are again equal (both rates being low).

Having established an evolutionary pattern of population change it is then possible to 'cluster' societies at different points on the curve. From subsequent analysis, three principal socio-economic groupings can then be identified—'traditional', underdeveloped societies of high growth potential and strongly associated with the early stages of the population curve; 'achieving' societies in a phase of transitional growth and located at or about the mid-point of the curve; and finally 'affluent', highly industrialised and developed societies clustered at the phase of incipient population decline.

Later research hypotheses based on the assumption that socio-economic groups can legitimately be segmented in the above manner have found broad acceptance. More importantly for the present study, a considerable research effort was subsequently directed to exploring possible correlations between socio-economic evolution and the formation of social character types, culminating in the identification of three basic character types clearly associated with the three principal stages of cultural, social and economic evolution (q.v.).

Studies of character type formation—linked to social and economic development—provide an ideal research base for a more systematic study of the nature and incidence of conspicuous consumption. If conspicuous consumption is a phenomenon created, as has been argued, by socio-cultural conditioning of individual consumer preferences then it will vary in type and intensity according to the society in which it occurs. Consequently, by looking more closely at the specific character conditioning effects of different social environments it should be possible, firstly, to draw some general conclusions about the expected implications with respect to conspicuous economic display, and subsequently to attempt a more empirical study of conspicuous consumption by building a data bank of information on observed patterns of conspicuous expenditures, duly segmented according to the social and economic conditions of the societies in which they occurred. As a first step, the distinctions between traditional, achieving and affluent societies need to be clearly drawn.

Traditional societies—those enjoying high growth potential but remaining relatively underdeveloped—reveal in their typical members a social character in which conformity to existing values is ensured by a strong tendency to follow tradition and which can therefore be categorised as 'tradition-directed'. In such societies, individual behaviour is shaped to a very large degree by static structures of status and power—structures which show little change over time and which are only slightly modified by successive generations. There is normally a rigid etiquette which is taught to children as soon as they are able to comprehend and which then plays an important part in shaping their behaviour patterns and in determining the actions and aspirations of a lifetime. The rigid traditions of such societies do not tolerate behaviour 'outside' the existing order of things and any behaviour which challenges the existing social order is punished within the system. The dominant culture provides ritual and routine to occupy and orient everyone and the opportunity given to an individual to pursue his personal aspirations is extremely limited. Life goals which can be considered to be the conscious choice of individuals are very limited, members of such societies are given a set of life goals by the traditions of the group to which they belong.

Individuality in behaviour in such societies is normally allowed only within families of very high status but even at this level individual expression is greatly constrained and must never be seen as challenging the system. The level of independent thought has necessarily to be restricted otherwise the philosophies on which the traditions of the society are based may come to be challenged, thus sowing the seeds of a radical realignment and reassessment of social norms and values.

Traditional underdeveloped societies of the type described are normally distinguished by characteristics which should heavily influence patterns of conspicuous consumption. Firstly, status is ascribed rather than achieved—that is, an individual is vested with social and economic power through inheritance, traditional office or family connection and not by way of personal, social or economic achievement. Social mobility is either totally absent or greatly restricted and people are expected to know their place within the social hierarchy and to behave accordingly. Secondly, the distribution of wealth is significantly unequal and should allow only a minority elite to conspicuously consume on any appreciable scale. Economic strength is necessarily a major determinant of ostentatious display and conspicuous consumption may well be undertaken only to display wealth with a view to confirming ascribed status. It is also true that the social status accorded to a few individuals in traditional societies is protected by ensuring a parallel economic strength which restricts the ability of lower status individuals to challenge the ruling power.

Given such a social and economic structure, we should expect that if conspicuous consumption is observed in traditional societies it will be undertaken primarily by a relatively small elite who enjoy inherited rights and status together with near total economic and political power. This conclusion, however, begs the question as to why people with monopoly social, economic and political power should be motivated to conspicuously consume. Two possible explanations exist in theory at least. Firstly, there may be a desire simply to flaunt power and to explicitly display the privileges of birth or office. Secondly, the society may be so organised that the privileged elite are required and expected by others to conspicuously consume or, perhaps more realistically, to spend conspicuously for the greater public good. These alternatives will be examined in detail at a later stage; for the moment, it is sufficient to note that conspicuous consumption in tradition-directed societies should theoretically find a narrow expression albeit at significantly high levels of expenditure.

The decay of feudalism and the subsequent collapse of traditional societies sees the emergence of transitional growth and of inner-directed social character types. Inner-directed societies are typically characterised by increased personal mobility, by a rapid accumulation of capital and by an almost constant expansion. Society comes to have far greater choices and gives scope for far greater levels of initiative. However, inner-directed individuals, although responding to changing social systems, are still directed to a large extent by a pattern of conformity which reflects the values of the 'old' society from which they have emerged. The social frame of reference is far wider and more flexible than in societies dependent on tradition-direction but, nevertheless, members are psychologically limited by 'voluntary' associations to which they tie themselves. In addition to family based traditions which are inevitably passed on to the individual, new traditions are developed as a result of the increasing division of labour and the stratification of society into new groupings. Hence, the individual still feels a need to stay within social norms even when historical tradition no longer rigidly controls his behaviour as in the case with earlier less developed societies.

In contrast to the static structure of many traditional communities, achieving societies allow far greater levels of social mobility and a more equal distribution of income and wealth. Individuals enjoy more independent thought and action and there is consequently a more generous definition of what is permissible social behaviour. Of particular importance is the fact that in those societies dominated by inner-direction, values can come to be translatable, at least in principle, into the impersonal standard of money. If money does indeed give value to all possessions and social position, then the attraction of conspicuous consumption should be heightened.

The dominant preoccupation of such societies is recognised as that of consumption. Increases in productivity—often spectacular—naturally increase peoples' abilities to consume, but the degree to which this consumption potential is channelled into conspicuous economic behaviour will be determined in large part by the corresponding stage of social development. At the earliest stages, when tradition-directed influences on social behaviour are still a considerable if diminishing force, the degree to which a redistribution of wealth prompts conspicuous consumption should be very small. However, as traditional values increasingly lose their authority and a new social order establishes itself, then the constraints on ostentatious display can be expected to diminish and a far higher level of conspicuous consumption emerge.

Ultimately, the degree to which conspicuous consumption is undertaken in high growth, inner-directed societies should be determined by how effective it is considered to be in securing an individual's status within society. The redistribution of income and wealth certainly should provide a greater opportunity for more people to conspicuously consume but individuals in such societies are thought to be motivated more by a struggle for self-approval rather than for public approval. Although there will be concern about what others may think and some need for their admiration, the inner-directed person is theoretically concerned with satisfying himself that he has achieved a lifestyle and life goals in which he can take pride. If this is so, it would suggest that the importance of conspicuous economic display could easily be overstated. Set against this, however, is the undoubted importance of money values and wealth symbolism in such societies—an importance which could require the 'successful' individual to seek self-approval in tangible form by converting his productive effort into a display of the wealth that it has brought him.

Societies which successfully pass through the phase of transitional growth eventually emerge as industrialised, affluent communities typified not only by declining birth and death rates but also by a particularly high per capita distribution of income and wealth. This 'affluent' society in turn has been seen to produce a third social character type which is other-directed rather than inner-directed and which is clearly a product of the social environment found in modern developed communities.

Individuals living in wealthy, industrialised countries may well enjoy material abundance and greater leisure but in a world which is increasingly centralised and bureaucratised and where all nations are brought into far greater contact with each other. Under such circumstances, it is argued, the inner-direction, self-assessment and enterprise of earlier, less affluent times becomes less and less relevant and it is increasingly other peoples' opinions and tastes which come to shape the individual's character and behaviour patterns. The scarcity-psychology of inner-direction is replaced by an abundance-psychology which inevitably influences social character and environment.

The concept of other-direction holds that an individual's contemporaries direct and shape his lifestyle and aspirations. The significant difference between inner- and other-directed societies is seen to lie in the fact that communication between individuals and groups is far stronger in the latter form of community where people are greatly influenced not only by their families and immediate personal friends but by 'media personalities' and by the mass of information, values and beliefs transmitted by the media in general. Behaviour is therefore largely conditioned by the views and standards of opinion leaders in society. The formerly all powerful influence of the nuclear and extended family and the desire to seek only self-assurance and respect is superceded by a new influence—that of the mass media and the views and values it transmits impersonally to its audience. Other-directed societies are typified by a sophisticated and highly developed communications network which serves to break down traditional forms of communication and influence and, in so doing, introduces a new form of conformity to the individual conformity to the opinions, beliefs, values and aspirations of media people and the media world.

The mass media is not only able to bring new ideas and cultural values to the attention of its audience but can also effectively cut across class boundaries to an extent which is impossible in less developed societies. Parents and class peers tend to lose their once undisputed role and their ability to ensure conformity with the views they seek to transmit to their family or class members is correspondingly diminished—a process which tends to reinforce media power and influence.

In parallel with the rise of media views and contemporary values, affluent societies offer to individuals a far higher level of education, literacy and intellectual debate than that found in traditional or developing communities. Thus the overall level and standard of communication is considerably improved. In such circumstances, it is argued, individuals must inevitably become far more concerned with other peoples' attitudes and values and will consequently ensure that their behaviour patterns conform with those laid down by the contemporary culture no matter how impermanent this may be.

At the theoretical level, conspicuous consumption could become far less attractive a proposition in other-directed societies. The high standards of education, literacy and economic welfare and the abundance psychology associated with general prosperity may combine to make conspicuous economic display relatively ineffective as a way to securing status gains. Indeed, material display could be a positive embarrassment rather than an advantage, more particularly if social groups and the media culture begin to reject or discount wealth as an indicator of social worth. Added to this, high levels of prosperity effectively 'devalue' wealth in so far that as a commodity it becomes relatively less scarce. In becoming more generally obtainable, money must inevitably lose some of its powers to impress.

There may exist a paradox whereby relative affluence allows—even seeks to promote—a high level of conspicuous consumption at the same time as a fundamental revision of attitudes towards wealth increasingly rejects materialism and ostentatious economic behaviour as a legitimate means to achieve status within the community. Any resultant reductions in the levels of conspicuous consumption, however, will be offset by the fact that the far greater numbers of people enjoying high discretionary incomes means that the opportunity for significant material display is extended to literally millions of individuals for the first time. These new consumers may well retain inner-directed aspirations and values in a predominantly other-directed society and continue to 'measure' social status in money terms. Conspicuous consumption could therefore continue at all social and economic levels and could possibly increase in overall importance rather than decline as a consumer preference.

Having identified three basic social systems and character types and the different patterns of conspicuous consumption that each could be expected to produce, it is important to recognise that these systems are not discreet in the sense that they can only exist within a society which is totally identified with one particular form of social organisation. It is still possible to find isolated societies which are wholly tradition-directed and which have no element of inner- or other-direction within them, but the vast majority of societies are able to embrace tradition, inner- and other-directed groups and to accommodate them within a cohesive social system. Any particular society may include those—perhaps in geographically isolated or economically underdeveloped and neglected regions—who find themselves at the bottom of the economic ladder and faced with little prospect of improvement within what may remain a regionally 'traditional' social system; those in more developed areas who live and work in a more 'open' social and economic environment and who enjoy a comfortable standard of living; and finally, those at the top of the socio-economic ladder who enjoy high levels of income and a relative abundance of capital assets. This mix of groups and sub-cultures will change continually in response to environmental changes and also as possible migration and general population movements bring people together who 'date' metaphorically from different points on the economic and social development scale.

Whilst many societies have such a mix of sub-systems, it should nevertheless be possible to identify in any society the particular character type which dominates national culture and general behaviour patterns and to categorise communities on this basis for the purposes of research—remembering at the same time that the terms 'traditional', 'achieving' and 'affluent' will refer to dominant rather than exclusive social characteristics.

Once societies are successfully stratified on the basis of dominant social and cultural norms, otherwise 'random' instances of conspicuous consumption can then be clustered and analysed in their appropriate social context. However, a further substantial problem of methodology remains in that subsequent research can be based either on empirical fieldwork which seeks to determine, at first hand, individual pre-purchase and post-purchase consumer motivation and opportunity, or on analysis of historical and secondary data. In so far as the study of conspicuous consumption is concerned, this choice of research method is again a difficult one to make.

The difficulties of attempting objective and reliable primary research into conspicuous behaviour at the individual level have to be acknowledged. A major problem in seeking to undertake a programme of empirical research lies in the fact that the conspicuous consumer, anxious to display wealth and gain in prestige, will rarely if ever explicitly admit to any such intentions. This is a rational decision on his part for any admission that money was or is being spent with a view to impressing others could produce an adverse reaction which would effectively nullify any possible gains from his expenditure. Societies in general insist that recognition and status are conferred upon but not overtly sought by individuals and it is therefore incumbent upon the status seeker to admit to no intention of 'buying' such recognition. Given the understandable reticence of conspicuous consumers, therefore, to admit that they are in fact purchasing for display, primary research becomes very difficult. Furthermore, if such research were to be carried out, the data obtained and the conclusions drawn would necessarily be highly subjective and open to wrong interpretation.

If it is not realistic to expect consumers to speak objectively about their conspicuous consumption intentions, an alternative solution to the problem of research methodology needs to be found. In essence, there is only one alternative approach—that is, to analyse such behaviour by observing various forms of ostentatious consumption as and when it occurs and by subsequently attempting to explain the motivations underlying such revealed behaviour. This approach immediately poses a further problem in that a subjective judgement has to be made by the researcher as to whether any observed purchase or consumption can and should be considered an act of conspicuous display. Whilst such assumptions can never be more than an informed value judgement based on a balance of probabilities, there is some considerable justification for adopting this research strategy.

The legitimacy of research by observation and report can be supported. Firstly, observations of uncontrolled actions and reactions are widely accepted as valid in both the physical and social sciences (this, of course, does not in itself prove legitimacy but does show that in choosing to identify and study conspicuous consumption in this way a research methodology is being used which already enjoys wide recognition). Secondly, conspicuous consumption itself is, by definition, exceptional consumer behaviour and must necessarily be 'conspicuous'. It seems reasonable, therefore, to allow the use of probability theory in deciding that a particular act of consumption can realistically be considered as conspicuous and ostentatious. In doing so, however, the purely statistical weakness of any such conclusion has to be recognised.

Any observed act of consumption will be justified in being considered primarily conspicuous if it can be reasonably assumed (i.e. if the balance of probabilities suggests) that display considerations dominated the decision to buy or consume. It has already been argued that two principal considerations may motivate the individual consumer—he may be purchasing a product either for the direct, tangible utility it is able to offer him or for the indirect utility gained through the reaction of others to the purchase. If direct utility is seen as by far the most important factor in his decision—and this will be true in the majority of cases—then, although there may be a 'conspicuous' element in the decision to spend or consume, the behaviour and buying motive can not be considered primarily conspicuous. In contrast, the pure conspicuous consumer will be not be at all interested in direct utility if he can be convinced that a particular product or act of consumption is effective or potentially effective as a means of displaying wealth and of therefore increasing status and prestige. If the product chosen for consumption is distinctive by its high cost, its conspicuous design, its social appeal and its ostentatious display in use, and shows at the same time a very limited practical utility value relative to its cost or to the price paid, then it is reasonable to suspect and believe that the consumption decision has been motivated primarily by display considerations.

Once the decision is taken to base research into conspicuous consumption on secondary reports and observation rather than on any primary investigation of individual motivations and intentions, a further problem remains—should the study be concerned with historical or with current report of such behaviour? To be most effective, studies of conspicuous consumption need to be carried out with reference to those communities in which a given type of social organisation is particularly dominant. In examining the patterns of conspicuous economic behaviour in societies categorised as traditional, for example, little can be learned from studying societies with traditional value systems which are rapidly being eroded by external pressure and communication from 'achieving' or 'affluent' communities. Similarly, research into achieving societies should be directed to communities in which the social and economic structure is such that traditional and affluent society influence is reduced to a minimum. By carefully selecting areas of research in this way it becomes far easier to 'match' patterns of conspicuous consumption with particular types of socio-economic organisation.

In so far as traditional societies are concerned, a historical research perspective is clearly preferable. It is becoming increasingly difficult, if not impossible, to identify and isolate present day communities which have not had their apparently dominant traditional values 'modified' often beyond recognition. By directing the research effort to historical observation, this problem of distortion is effectively removed. Data on traditional societies is therefore best obtained by reference to the work of social anthropologists who, whilst never wholly concerned with conspicuous consumption per se, have frequently observed and commented on the role and importance of ostentatious economic display in such communities.

Similarly, with regard to achieving societies, it is particularly important to screen out the effects of modern international communications in transmitting affluent society values and norms to such communities and this task becomes impossible if research is attempted into achieving societies of the present day. Again, historical analysis effectively removes this communications problem and allows conspicuous consumption to be examined in societies in which inner-directed character types are clearly dominant.

Finally, and in contrast, studies into the nature and incidence of conspicuous economic display in affluent societies must necessarily be carried out with reference to current observation and report. Affluent societies are an entirely recent phenomenon and a progression from achieving societies in which substantial reserves of capital and wealth are created and accumulated. Societies have only been recognised as affluent in this sense for some few years and research data must therefore relate either to present day or immediate past experience. In some ways, of course, research into current behaviour is often more difficult and subjective in that the observer may himself be conditioned by the society which he is observing; however, a considerable amount of information is already available for use as acceptable reference material in the study of affluent society conspicuous consumption.

In the following chapters an attempt is made to analyse conspicuous consumption within this more formal research framework. In Chapter 4 conspicuous economic behaviour is examined in the context of traditional societies and is identified in both primitive and feudal types of social organisation. The view of conspicuous consumption in primitive traditional communities is broadly based on the random observations of social anthropologists, whilst analysis of economic display in feudal societies is more specific and relates predominantly to the European experience from 1000–1700 AD. Chapter 5 is concerned with the nature and incidence of conspicuous consumption in achieving societies and concentrates exclusively on the 'classic' nineteenth century and early twentieth century experiences of the United States and of Britain. Finally, Chapter 6 looks at the motives and opportunities for conspicuous consumption in modern affluent societies and identifies the fundamental changes in social and economic attitudes which have contrived to produce new forms of this exceptional consumer behaviour.

Notes

Research into the nature and incidence of conspicuous consumption is particularly difficult to organise. Firstly, it is a form of consumer behaviour which is significantly and extraordinarily determined by the interplay of social, cultural and economic factors and which ideally requires multi-variate analysis of a most complex kind. Secondly, conspicuous consumption is difficult to identify and isolate. Status-directed economic display is never discussed (except in others) or knowingly revealed and does not, therefore, lend itself to controlled statistical analysis even should such an approach be possible.

Acknowledging these major difficulties, it becomes necessary to limit the research objectives of any preliminary study. Societies can usefully be segmented only in broad terms in order to obtain a base frame of reference and there must inevitably be some resort to generalisation in seeking to explain different patterns of conspicuous consumption.

With respect firstly to segmentation, socio-economic differentiation is not of itself sufficient for conspicuous consumption research. A link has to be made between culture, socio-economic structure and social character formation. In this respect, the work of Riesman (*The Lonely Crowd*, Yale University Press, 1950) clearly offers the most appropriate research base and has been adopted—and adapted—to suit the needs of the present study.

Secondly, whilst conceding the advantages of research into specific individual behaviour, an eloquent defence of generalised research within a comparative frame of reference was put forward by McClelland in the preface to his work on the *Achieving Society* (Van Nostrand, New York, 1961). A similar defence would be proposed for this study of conspicuous consumption behaviour in its various forms.

4 Conspicuous consumption in traditional societies

One of the distinctive features of many primitive traditional societies was their lack of any significant social and economic stratification. In essence, a form of communism prevailed in which all members of the community were treated as equals and where individuals were expected to display no wish to appear 'superior' to other members of the group.

The majority of these societies were organised around subsistence economies and no economic 'surplus' existed within the community. However, if surpluses did by chance build up they were expected to be distributed in order to raise the overall subsistence level. If this was not done and wealth accumulated with one individual, he was often publicly ridiculed for being a 'wealthy man'—an insulting term. Wealth display was similarly rejected and any individual seeking to promote his own economic superiority was roundly condemned.[1]

In such communities the social system was carefully organised to make any individual attempt at conspicuous consumption unprofitable in economic, social and political terms. Group homegeneity was assiduously developed. Firstly, the organisation of economic activity ensured that no really significant wealth differences could build up between individuals and the opportunity to conspicuously consume was therefore always kept to a minimum. Secondly, wealth itself was not regarded as being at all symbolic of high status and prestige. The display of individual wealth was typically greeted with considerable hostility, being taken as a sign that the person in question had not been as generous as he should have been to the community at large. Indeed, in certain societies, status was actually increased if material benefits and possessions

47

were deliberately refused; to this end, customs of gift giving developed to ensure that all goods of value moved in a slow flowing current among individuals and that no one person kept anything of particular value very long.[2]

In societies based on primitive communism, economic surpluses could not be allowed to concentrate in the hands of a few individuals who enjoyed a separate and superior status. Cultures and sub-cultures whose preservation depended on equality of social status and of wealth distribution naturally attacked movement towards conspicuous economic display. As traditional societies evolved, however, cultural values changed and created environments which allowed greater recognition of individual self-interest. 'Developed' traditional societies which had moved away from primitive communism tended to adopt a far more stratified social and economic system. There was usually a significantly greater inequality not only of income and wealth distribution but also of social status and prestige. Social mobility was at the time restricted to protect the incumbents of high office and to ensure that the ascribed status system normally predominant in such societies was maintained without threat.

The strongest status claims in these communities came from sex, age and biological relationships. Social class influences supplemented these but in essence each social class group had its own sex, age and family statuses and was really a microcosm of the large social unit. Ascribed status dominated the social system and although there was sometimes room for a little achieved status—to serve as incentives for socially acceptable behaviour or as escapes for the individual—this was never great enough to allow a significant number of people with no ascribed status to gain positions of power within the system.[3]

In the hierarchical society with a clearly defined social and economic pyramid, economic surpluses were no longer distributed equally within the community but tended to gravitate upwards into the possession of the ruling elites. Payments and tributes were made to chiefs either as an unquestioned 'perk' of office or to ensure that they did not have to work for their living. Many products of value automatically became the property of rulers regardless of who had worked to manufacture or obtain them. And, in addition to compulsory acquisition, surpluses often needed to be paid as tribute to obtain preferential treatment and favours.[4]

In societies where wealth was accumulated by those in positions of social and economic power and in which status was ascribed rather than achieved, the resultant economic surplus could be disposed of in one of three principal ways—it could be hoarded (or conspicuously saved), publicly redistributed through charities, feasts and ceremonies, or conspicuously destroyed. Each of these three alternatives merits some separate consideration and explanation.

Conspicuous saving was socially profitable in those communities in which it was the actual possession of wealth and not its display through conspicuous consumption which was most important in conferring status. Ascribed status in such societies could be reinforced by a person's prosperity but this wealth was not for public announcement through excessive ostentation. Although it was often quite acceptable to spend significantly at such ceremonies as weddings and funerals, the dignity of privileged elites was protected only by a corresponding dignity of possession and display.[5]

Wealth could most readily be hoarded in those societies whose culture and overall social environment made it impossible to secure additional status through conspicuous economic display—i.e. societies in which social position was unequivocally ascribed on the basis of tradition and heredity. Many parts of India, for example, had (indeed still have) a social caste system in which status was determined primarily on hereditary group membership based on traditional occupation and sectarian affiliation. In these conditions, wealth could not buy an improvement in social position for a very clear distinction was made between 'status'—usually associated with religious supremacy—and 'power' pertaining to the temporal and materialistic. The display of wealth, therefore, could secure power but not increase status which derived exclusively from non-material factors.[6]

Socially sanctioned wealth hoarding tended to suppresss conspicuous consumption for two main reasons. Firstly, the owners of wealth—those in a position to conspicuously consume—had no incentive to spend or distribute their material surplus. Secondly, the act of hoarding itself ensured that no redistribution of wealth could take place, thus offering no opportunity to those lower down the social hierarchy to indulge in display expenditures. Furthermore, the overall lack of wealth redistribution in such societies meant that the rate of economic growth was often negligible, a fact which tended to maintain and reinforce the existing social and economic order.

Whilst wealth accumulation secured status in some traditional communities, it was more common to find societies demanding a significant redistribution of wealth away from those elites who came to possess it in the first instance. The economic surplus still accumulated with a privileged social group but they in turn were expected to spend conspicuously in the 'public interest' to meet social and economic obligations imposed on them by the positions and offices they enjoyed. The excess earned by the community as a whole, therefore, was redistributed by the elites in the form of feasts, ceremonies, gift exchange or alms giving.

The many forms such redistribution could take are well documented. Most widely observed were the various 'potlatch' ceremonies which were institutionalised in many societies throughout the world. Potlatch—a North American Indian word now used generically by social anthropologists—refers to the ceremony of public distribution of goods and was first identified among four peoples of the American North West—the Haida, Tlingit, Tsimshian and Kwakiutl. Similar behaviour patterns have been recorded in traditional societies of all continents. The potlatch system existed to allow goods to be given away in return for increased social status. Those who received the goods at feasts and other ceremonies disposed of their utilitarian value whilst those who gave them renounced that utilitarian value in favour of status consolidation or improvement. The purpose of the potlatch was, therefore, to assert social standing and compete for higher and higher prestige and, in those societies which condoned or expected such behaviour, the ritual was institutionalised. Recipients at a potlatch had no choice as to whether they accepted the goods and gifts offered; they were obliged to do so by custom. Similarly, the donors were assured of status rewards by their 'generosity'.[7]

In the earlier non-money societies, potlatch rituals centred primarily on food distribution and gift giving of various sorts, but the custom (or obligation) often survived the introduction of money as the basic measure of wealth. Whereas the more primitive societies expected prestige (as opposed to subsistence) foods to be distributed by local leaders, later money-based societies simply transferred the source of prestige away from food and towards money or money earning raw materials and products—even to imported goods, purchased with money by the ruling social and economic hierarchy.

Public redistribution of wealth from social and economic elites to the less privileged members of a particular community played a most important role in many traditional societies and was used as a mechanism both to secure the status and position of those at the top of the social hierarchy and to ensure that the rewards of productive effort were enjoyed by all members of the community. Factors of social obligation or canons of ritual often entered into economic transactions and nowhere was this better observed than in the potlatch-type ceremonies which have occurred in all parts of the world.[8] The greatest moral obligation incumbent on leaders of many traditional societies was that of giving material aid to their people and ceremonially equalising goods distribution. Indeed, if they failed to do so they were often threatened by social 'inferiors' who may have been able to accumulate some reserves of a particular commodity. Such people, by distributing this more limited wealth, could gradually gain prestige through distributive activities and wean loyalty and support away from social leaders.[9]

In total contrast to public redistribution of wealth which directly or indirectly benefited all members of a particular community, an entirely negative variation of the potlatch tradition, based on the concept of 'conspicuous destruction', was adopted in certain societies to secure status and prestige. Unlike feasts and ceremonies in which some direct utility was gained from consumption of the food or goods on offer, the public destruction of wealth offered direct utility to no individual. However, it seems to have been adopted by certain social elites to achieve the same basic respect for status and position by demonstrating an ability to 'throw away' wealth with contempt for its value. When goods were completely destroyed, their utilitarian value was eliminated but converted into social, ceremonial or ritual value which added to the status of the destroyer.

The conspicuous destruction of food has perhaps been most commonly reported and observed. The culture of Western Pacific Trobriand Islanders, for example, allowed chiefs to store vast quantities of yams which were meant only for display. This food supply was then deliberately not used until it went rotten and was then thrown very conspicuously on the community rubbish dump.[10] Many other such societies adopted similar rituals in which articles of considerable value were deliberately destroyed by those rich enough to stand the loss of such wealth. The status gain came from the ability of the individual to show a level of wealth high enough to allow him to treat with contempt articles which had a very real value to others and which would certainly never have been wilfully destroyed by them.

The conspicuous destruction of goods was often used in another form as an overt rivalry gesture between two or more individuals who were competing with each other for status and position. Under the 'rules of the game' one party was required to deliberately destroy something of high value and challenge the other individual or individuals to destroy something of equal value or to be shamed into conceding status inferiority. Unlike conspicuous destruction undertaken to secure deference in those of inferior social position, however, this 'competitive' destruction was intended to determine relative status rankings between individuals who shared or competed for prestige at the same social level.

Hoarding, public redistribution and conspicuous destruction may all have been acceptable forms of behaviour in their appropriate social contexts but how far can such behaviour be classified as conspicuous consumption as it has been defined—i.e. the ostentatious display of material prosperity to achieve status gains? Hoarding or conspicuous saving has little if anything in common with conspicuous consumption apart from the fact that both are concerned with securing social position and prestige. Conspicuous public expenditure certainly owes something to a belief in ostentatious display as a necessary element in achieving and retaining high social rank but it could not properly be classed as a 'pure' form of conspicuous consumption, the former being undertaken in the belief that it is generosity which secures status whilst the latter assumes that the conspicuous display of wealth—usually demonstrated by excessive personal consumption of goods and services—is sufficient in itself to gain the admiration, respect and deference of others. Finally, and perhaps more positively, conspicuous destruction does seem to have a stronger affinity with conspicuous consumption in so far as it is intended to secure recognition and status for individuals who enjoy considerable wealth and who display their material (and by implication social) superiority by ceremonially destroying a part of this wealth in public.

Conspicuous destruction is perhaps the ultimate expression of that total disregard for cost and value which Veblen referred to as 'conspicuous waste'. Whilst not universally observed, it occurred in a sufficient number of traditional societies to be considered an early if primitive illustration of an attitude to wealth which runs counter to many 'rational' economic theories of individual resource management under conditions of scarcity. Wealth accumulation as an economic and social aim may therefore only be understood in certain societies if due recognition is given to status and prestige considerations with which wealth formation and subsequent expenditure are inextricably linked. It is often assumed that man ultimately wants to maximise money gains or increase wealth only to increase his ability to purchase or command resources which offer him a direct physical utility. Such an assumption can not be justified in respect of communities in which personal reputation may be determined by an individual's propensity for wasting assets and resources at a faster and higher rate than his peers.

If conspicuous destruction alone can be considered close to 'pure' conspicuous consumption, then it would appear that traditional societies—at their earlier more basic stages of development—were remarkable by the overall lack of conspicuous wealth display in so far as such display was focused on profligate personal consumption of goods and services. However, the reasons for this apparent lack of conspicuous consumer behaviour were self-evident in most societies of the type. Firstly, the power structures were such that status was predominantly ascribed and normally could not be 'bought' by individuals seeking to improve their social standing. Wealth could be used only to reinforce a status level which had already been awarded in other ways. Secondly, individual status in traditional communities lacking an organised political or military elite was a status conferred voluntarily either through social custom or by common consent of the members of such societies. Although ascribed status was reasonably secure, it was granted only on the understanding that the individual acknowledged the obligations associated with high rank. These obligations often included a clear understanding that wealth in material possessions was never to be overtly displayed and that the office holder had to pursue a policy of conspicuous saving. Again, there was often a strongly imposed obligation to distribute accrued wealth to the public at large through various ceremonies and rituals.

Implicit in such duties and obligations was the belief that wealth accumulated by economic or social elites could not be spent by these privileged classes exclusively for their own material comfort or private consumption. Under such constraints, it is not altogether surprising to find little evidence of conspicuous consumption for status gain; it would appear that the only sanctioned form of such behaviour—and this only in certain societies—was the conspicuous destruction of wealth already referred to. It is perhaps paradoxical that such destructive behaviour is in itself the most extreme form of conspicuous consumption yet was evident in traditional societies which condemned other less extreme forms of ostentatious economic display.

The absence of a high level of conspicuous consumption in primitive communities stands in marked contrast to the incidence of such behaviour which has been observed and recorded in more 'advanced' (yet still traditional) societies. Historically, a significant feature of developing communities was the growth of a political and military power which was normally used by ascribed status office holders to consolidate their social and economic ascendancy. Once political and military power became entrenched with the ruling hierarchy, the opportunity for conspicuous consumption became far greater, primarily because status—albeit still predominantly ascribed—could be secured without the continuing consent of the community from which it originally derived. A situation therefore arose in which wealth in the form of an economic surplus was still transmitted upwards to a socially privileged minority who now had no immediate obligation (other than perhaps a moral one which could be and often was effectively discounted) to treat these accruals in a way approved by the society at large.

Examination of European social history from 1000 to 1700 provides perhaps the best evidence of the values and behaviour of these 'second stage' traditional societies. The feudal systems which arose in the early Middle Ages and persisted in modified form through to the eighteenth century represented the fusion of ascribed status with military strength and political power. The period was often remarkable for the inordinately high levels of conspicuous consumption—for both 'horizontal' (within-group) and 'vertical' (between-group) status gains—which were undertaken by the ruling minorities and by those at the top of the social hierarchy who supported and sustained them.

Throughout the period 1000–1700 the population of Europe was comparatively static and for long periods did not grow at all.[11] When it did, the rate of increase was always very low. Income and wealth distribution were grossly unequal and society was clearly divided between the rich and the poor. The inequality of wealth was greater than that of income because of the very great concentration of land and other property in the hands of the nobility and the church. As in more primitive, earlier societies, these inequalities resulted from the compulsory or 'voluntary' transfer of wealth and income by levy, duties and taxation. The elites did redistribute some of these economic surpluses in the form of feasts and ceremonies or, more commonly, as donations to charities but the actual degree of real redistribution was significantly less than it could have been.

Taxation was used to concentrate a large share of available resources in the hands of the socially privileged but only a small percentage of these funds were redistributed downwards—a far smaller percentage, in fact, than that commonly observed in less developed traditional societies where large scale redistribution was often socially mandatory. Public feasts were organised but lavish expenditure on these was reserved for those occasions of particularly symbolic value from which the organisers could directly benefit—e.g. to celebrate the visit of a fellow dignitary—and most of the benefits of such feasts were in reality enjoyed by those already rich. In so far as charity was concerned, various family budgets of the rich and the well off in the sixteenth century show 'ordinary charity' of the order of one to five per cent of consumption expenditure but a large part of this charity was actually a transfer of wealth to the church which then gave out to the poor only a small part of what it had received.[12] Indeed, the church itself was throughout this period a major conspicuous consumer in its own right. It amassed an immense fortune and 'at the apex of the structure, the expenditure of the papal court had all the characteristics of the conspicuous display of a lavishly rich princely court'.[13]

As early as the twelfth century, charity had become institutionalised and every aristocrat primarily used the money he collected for two ends—sacrifice (to God and to the church) and adornment. There were few individuals of any standing who did not found a collegiate church or support a monastery. Pious gifts headed the list of expenses and by this time, significantly, it was money rather than material goods which was given.[14]

In so far as adornment was concerned, spending was focused on food, on clothes and on housing. The range of opportunities for conspicuous expenditure was naturally far narrower than is true of the present day. The economic system and the state of the arts did not offer the richer consumer the great variety of products and services which characterise modern industrial societies. The basic difference, in fact, between the rich and the poor was that the poor did not have enough money to buy any significant quantities of food and clothing or to invest in housing, whereas the rich spent extravagantly on all three.[15]

Attitudes towards wealth and income from the tenth century onwards encouraged a high level of conspicuous consumption. Productive investment of funds was socially frowned upon because it was not in keeping with the teaching of the church that money should not be used

54

to make more money. Lacking any socially approved opportunity for investment, therefore, the wealthy consumed heavily. Significant outlays on food, clothing and palatial houses, together with money spent in maintaining a large personal retinue (a factor used to judge a man's status throughout the period) did, however, help to provide employment and to redistribute capital to some extent but never as efficiently as direct investment in production would have done.[16]

If economic surpluses remained after all conspicuous consumption needs had been met, the wealthy were obliged to save or to hoard them. In pre-industrial Europe, two major factors favoured the freezing of savings in the form of hoarding. Firstly, institutions to collect savings and to direct them to productive uses were either lacking or totally inadequate. Secondly, the opportunities for turning savings to productive purposes were themselves limited. Such circumstances, together with the church's disapproval of the productive use of income, combined to ensure that the amount of hoarding over these centuries was massive in times of high economic surplus. The overall long term effect, however, was significantly reduced by the extended periods of dis-hoarding entered into by the nobility when the demands of their conspicuous expenditures could not adequately be met out of income.

It is difficult to identify distinct patterns of conspicuous consumption within the period 1000–1700 but some broad differentiation can be made. The period 1000–1200 was one in which the overriding consideration of the wealthy was to spend conspicuously to 'buy' followers and peasant workers.[17] Success and wealth were measured primarily by the number of people in a rich man's entourage. Property was wealth and much emphasis was naturally given to the ownership of land and people. From 1200–1500 the power of the church was greatly increased and consolidated and the concept of 'conspicuous charity' was introduced and encouraged by most religious orders. Non-charitable conspicuous consumption, however, continued to focus on seigneurial courts and on food and clothing expenditure.[18]

By 1500 the absolute power of the ruling elites was diminishing. In England, for example, the old feudal nobility lost most of its real power after the Wars of the Roses and the first Tudor king and his entourage had to listen seriously to the wishes and preferences of the nation's chief subjects. The merchant class was starting to develop and taxes were controlled—even lowered—causing a substantial check to the sums of money that had previously been transferred in great quantities to the ruling elites. Economic surpluses were more evenly distributed in that a new elite—agricultural and property owning landlords—became a significant social, economic and political force and began to adopt high levels of conspicuous consumption on fine houses and country estates.[19]

Another factor which had ensured a significant redistribution of surpluses from the thirteenth century onwards was the increasing need to control and administer a social and economic system which had become far more complex and difficult to manage. The necessary establishment of royal exchequers, chanceries and law courts meant that there were many more civil servants to be 'looked after'. In addition, private armies were frequently recruited and used either for offensive or defensive purposes and these too required a substantial financial tribute for services rendered and for continued loyalty.

In summary, the European experience from 1000–1700 was such that conspicuous consumption on the part of the nobility and other social elites could and did prosper. However, whilst the marriage of ascribed status and power gave added impetus to conspicuous economic behaviour over the period, there was one factor of continuing significance which effectively differentiated such feudal societies from the earlier traditional communities of the type already examined. Throughout the period, the political and military authority enjoyed by the elites had to be consolidated and sustained and this required that those individuals who actively supported the power structure be rewarded for their loyalty and effort. Consequently, much of the wealth accruing to the rulers and aristocracies in such societies had increasingly and necessarily to be redistributed not only to the community as a whole but perhaps more importantly to the senior governors, administrators and bureaucrats who ensured the survival and wellbeing of the existing social and economic system.

In more advanced feudal societies this financial and material tribute could be so great that a sizeable part of the economic surplus of the community which could potentially be given to personal conspicuous consumption by the ruling class was channelled to others as a reward for maintaining the system and for securing the power base of the rulers. Under conditions such as these, significant levels of conspicuous consumption could be observed at two levels. Certainly the ruling elite made great show of their affluence and consumed ostentatiously, but conspicuous economic opportunities were increasingly given to those individuals—whether soldiers, administrators or bureaucrats—who preserved and protected the existing order. The medieval 'courts' and the privileges and wealth their members enjoyed were to some extent the price paid by rulers for the ultimate power that was conferred on them by ascribed status but, more importantly, that was maintained against threat from outside by the governing administrative, legal and military authorities. The price was often so great, in fact, that the overall economic surplus was quickly consumed and, when opportunities for dis-hoarding had been exhausted, ways were constantly being sought to increase revenues and taxes to ensure that a conspicuous standard of living could be maintained by the strategic elite.

The pattern of conspicuous consumption in Europe during some seven hundred years of feudalism showed the changes of emphasis and direction which have already been noted. In essence, the early unfettered ability of the elites to indulge in ostentatious display and self-aggrandisement was slowly tempered by the realities of political and economic changes which required a more sensitive distribution of the economic surplus.

This pattern of development was by no means unique to medieval Europe. If we examine another traditional society incorporating the same feudal and highly structured system—that of Rome between the third century BC and the third century AD—a similar interpretation of conspicuous economic behaviour can be made. At the beginning of the period, nobles had traditionally adopted a relatively frugal lifestyle. There was a greater eagerness to acquire riches rather than to spend them. However, as their elitist position became more secure, they turned increasingly to conspicuous expenditure and consumption for both 'vertical' status consolidation and 'horizontal' status gains. This ostentatious display soon seemed to be growing in geometric progression.[20] Gladiatorial shows, for example, were originally introduced as funeral games: the first recorded instance in 264 BC involved only three pairs of gladiators but by 216 BC twenty-two pairs were used and by 174 BC seventy-four pairs in a celebration lasting three days. The level of aristocratic consumption generally was increasing to fabulous proportions and the financial pressures created by the status requirements of the rich led the authorities to introduce sumptuary laws to prevent the self-destruction of the social elite.[21] (Similar laws were introduced in medieval Europe to dampen down excessive levels of conspicuous display.) The major area of conspicuous expenditure at this time was on ostentatious villas and property but absurd prices were also paid for decorations and articles of vertu of many different kinds.[22]

The high levels of expenditure achieved by Roman nobility were possible only because the equites (businessmen) of the period accumulated high surpluses which were heavily taxed. Apart from personal conspicuous consumption, the only call on aristocratic wealth at this time was the bribery of the urban proletariats by means of which the nobility maintained a political and social ascendancy.[23] This was achieved by spending generously on public feasts and festivals and by organising a comprehensive programme of amusements. This high level of public expenditure survived the transition from republic to monarchy when a Minister of Amusement was appointed to set up free public festivals. The provincial nobility in turn imitated Rome's ostentation and paid for games and entertainments or built places of amusement.[24]

Matching developments which were to occur in Europe over one thousand years later, the level of wealth concentration with the nobility eventually began to decline as the demands of effectively 'managing' the later Empire required the appointment and reward of competent administrators. The economic surplus was partially redistributed for reasons of political survival and those who supported the state—bureaucrats, businessmen and soldiers—came to expect and demand a share of the great wealth which had hitherto been concentrated in a few hands. Rather than secure their position by seeking to placate the proletariat directly through high expenditure on public shows and spectacles, the ruling oligarchy shifted the direction of wealth redistribution away from the masses and towards the strategic elites who were prepared to sustain them in power.[25]

Most historical evidence suggests that in the more advanced yet traditional societies the power of feudal monarchs or aristocracies to spend excessively and without due regard for the realities of political, military and economic life could only be sustained over a limited period of time. Whilst feudalism depended on suppression, those who suppressed others in the interests of the ruling parties eventually came to demand a share of the wealth they helped to secure. However, wealth redistribution was not always necessary. In societies where economic development was minimal or totally absent and where the political and social status quo was under no threat, ruling elites were able to sustain enormous levels of conspicuous consumption over many centuries. The feudal structure which emerged in India after the sixth century AD gave rise to a status-power elite which expropriated surplus wealth through 'jajmani'—a complicated system of levies and taxes—and used this surplus not to invest in production or trade but 'to squander on extravagent urban living, monuments and temples'.[26] These conspicuous excesses continued virtually unabated into the twentieth century and were sustained largely because of the total inflexibility of a caste system which refused to question traditional, God-given values and allowed no stimulus to political, social or economic reform. Again, religious beliefs—reinforced by the very high status given to priests—controlled the range of consumption more strictly for all castes.[27]

In looking for an explanation of the persistence of high levels of exclusive, aristocratic conspicuous consumption in India, one fact would appear to be of particular significance. Because status was totally ascriptive, the motivation to conspicuously consume could only have been vicarious and intended to flaunt the privileges of total power. It could not have been undertaken to make any status gains because, under the Indian caste system, the hierarchic gradation of status was absolutely distinct from the gradation of power. The Brahman (or priest) who consecrated the power of the rulers and of the dominant castes ranked above kings and princes in terms of status, even though he was materially dependent on those who enjoyed real economic power. Conversely, whilst kings and princes were materially 'superior' to the priests, they were subordinate to them in spiritual and status terms. Both priests and rulers realised their interdependence and were mutually supporting.[28]

Therefore, whilst the growth of strategic, administrative elites in Europe and elsewhere allowed senior bureaucrats and soldiers to hope to secure new status gains through the accumulation and subsequent display of wealth, this opportunity was totally denied in India and served to channel any conspicuous behaviour exclusively into competition within rather than between castes. As a by-product, it ensured that the extravagances of Moghul India's rulers continued unabated and unchallenged over the centuries. Indeed, these conspicuous economic excesses continued as far as the British colonial period and the lifestyles of Indian elites were recognised by the British as clearly surpassing those of the European aristocracies of the period. Many European elites could have wished for caste systems similar to those which sustained the Indian rulers in such absolute power and wealth.[29]

A summary review of the nature and development of other feudal societies suggests that they approximated either to the European or the Indian 'models' outlined above—that is, they were either relatively short lived or endured in original form over many centuries, depending on the values and social structures of the primitive traditional societies from which they derived. This would suggest, therefore, that it is possible not only to distinguish broadly between 'early' and 'advanced' forms of traditional society but also between different forms both of first stage (primitive) and second stage (feudal) communities.

What conclusions can therefore be drawn from the analysis to date? Firstly, traditional societies were typified by hierarchical social structures, by marginal changes in population and by a clear concentration of wealth at the top of the social pyramid. The opportunity for high levels of conspicuous consumption was reserved for the privileged elite in such communities but the motivation to consume in this way seems to have varied according to the effective power structure operating within the society. When status and power were separated and social rank awarded on an ascriptive basis without conferring any corresponding political or military rights, then conspicuous consumption undertaken for purely personal prestige reasons seems to have been very limited—primarily because status awards carried obligations with respect to economic behaviour which had to be met if an individual's social position was to be maintained. In contrast, when political power was also given to—or taken by—those whose ascribed status was high in any particular community, historical evidence suggests that levels of conspicuous economic display as a means of status reinforcement became particularly high as the alliance of economic and political power allowed the ruling hierarchy to renege on any social obligations on which their ascribed status privileges once depended.

It is clearly not possible to offer a universal theory of conspicuous consumption in so far as traditional communities based on ascribed status are concerned. What can be claimed is that the concentration of wealth in all such societies was in itself a necessary but certainly not a sufficient condition for high absolute levels of conspicuous consumption. Ostentatious display for personal status gain was often culturally unacceptable and only appeared at significant levels when strategic power enabled the individual who enjoyed high social and economic status to effectively ignore or override the cultural objections to such behaviour. Secondly, there was a marked difference in the incidence of such behaviour in primitive yet 'democratic' traditional communities and in the autocratic, feudal societies which often developed out of such communities as all forms of power concentrated in the hands of the social elite.

The analysis to date has focused only on the incidence of conspicuous consumption among those fortunate enough, by dint of their ascribed status, to enjoy relatively high levels of income or wealth. Of equal importance is the incidence of such behaviour among those lower down the social scale who were economically deprived in relative terms but who may nevertheless have conspicuously consumed within their more limited resources. Whilst most historical and anthropological research has tended to concentrate on the luxury expenditure and consumption of the economically privileged, there is some data available on economic display behaviour at other socio-economic levels in traditional communities.

Low status members of a society in which there was a predetermined and independent social ranking system based on ascribed status had no real opportunity of improving their social standing through conspicuous consumption. Even when limited opportunities for status improvement did exist, the concentration of wealth with those already enjoying social and material privilege made it impossible for 'commoners' to reach a required level of ostentatious expenditure. Given these restrictions in terms of 'vertical' social movement, low status individuals could only channel any social aspirations they may have had into their relationships with others of the same social class or group. The question now arises as to the extent to which these 'horizontal' aspirations found expression in conspicuous consumption behaviour and what evidence there is suggests that such consumption in its pure form—that is, as a simple display of wealth to secure within-group status gains—often existed on a quite significant scale.

Conspicuous display at low status levels occurred firstly in a modified form in which—and unlike conspicuous consumption undertaken by those who were really wealthy in relative and absolute terms—there was no significant element of economic 'waste' associated with such behaviour. Various patterns of consumption allowed this cost minimising display which was peculiarly adapted to the needs of the economically disadvantaged. Firstly, there were many societies which allowed status gains to be made by those who used what wealth they possessed for the private entertaining of guests and visitors from within the same social stratum.[30] Such entertainments and hospitality could be organised either by those who had already achieved a certain status within the group or by those who were still seeking to secure it. Visitors were greatly indulged at such ceremonies and large quantities of valuable food and other goods could be conspicuously given in entertainment. However, such lavish expenditure would normally have been impossible to sustain for any period of time and a mechanism existed to ensure that this display was not, in fact, a real cost to the consumer. To this end, visitors were morally and socially obliged to give a fully equivalent amount back to the host on a subsequent occasion or to lose status as a forfeit. This 'reciprocal entertaining' therefore served as a source of status conference yet at no significant net cost to the participants—it was essentially a cost effective derivative of the 'wasteful' conspicuous consumption observed at the higher levels of such societies.

Studies carried out into the workings of the Indian caste system have also shown a variation of conspicuous consumption which was employed by members of nearly all caste groups as a means of improving their social position within the caste. The ostentatious display of wealth could come significantly high in the budget of the poorest families and jewels, bracelets, etc. were openly 'consumed'. However, apart from the initial investment in such goods, this again was a no-cost modification of conspicuous economic behaviour—or more correctly a derivative of conspicuous saving—in that, although it was often the entire wealth of a family which was displayed in ornaments instead of being inconspicuously hoarded or saved, it was clearly not on display with any intention of consuming or reducing a long term social and economic asset.[31]

Whilst no-cost modifications of conspicuous consumption occurred in many early societies, there was also a considerable degree of wasteful conspicuous consumption which was deemed socially necessary at all levels of society if status gains were to be made or past gains to be consolidated. In nearly all traditional communities, high levels of conspicuous expenditure were expected and required at two central events in the lives of all families—at weddings and at funerals. Marriages called for inordinate levels of expenditure, firstly in the form of dowries or bride-price and secondly to ensure that the wedding ceremony was distinguished by its generosity and by its financial profligacy. Many people, in fact, borrowed large sums of money or equivalent goods and services to meet their social obligations in so far as the marriages of their children were concerned and there is little doubt that the principal reason for such high expenditure lay in the fact that considerable status gains could be and were made by behaving in a generous and wasteful manner on such occasions. Similarly, funerals and funeral ceremonies were normally marked by a high degree of conspicuous display and elaborate preparations were made to ensure that the immediate community was able to observe the time, effort and money which had been put into the act of proper burial or cremation. Whilst there could be assumed to have been genuine grief at the death of a family member and an acknowledged status-free obligation to see the dead well provided for, it was equally true that conspicuous expenditure on funerals allowed considerable status gains to be made by the consumers.

Conspicuous consumption at lower status levels of traditional societies acted as a safety valve in that it gave individuals who had no real opportunity of making progress to higher social classes or groups the chance of satisfying a basic need for status and position. To ensure social peace and order, individuals were given the opportunity to seek a better ranking at the particular social 'level' to which they were confined by ascribed status. This opportunity could only be given by allowing advances in social standing on the basis of factors over which the individual had control and the discretionary use of assets—whether on a net-cost or no-cost basis—was clearly suitable for the purpose.

It is interesting to note that predominantly ascribed-status societies could not allow status movement and status related behaviour at lower socio-economic levels without permitting some form of achieved status system to operate. However, ascriptive societies were always well aware of the social need which existed at all levels of the community to improve personal prestige and social standing and allowed this element of achieved status seeking to function without significant restriction. It is difficult, if not impossible, to identify a society in which status was totally ascribed both between and within all social levels for, whilst 'vertical' movement was always suppressed, 'horizontal' competition for status gains on the basis of personal achievement acted as a release for status aspirations and so served to preserve and protect the dominant ascribed-status elites.

The above analysis of conspicuous consumption in traditional societies offers some insight into the motivations and opportunities for such behaviour in the earliest forms of social and economic community. However, it is important that such studies are not taken to be of interest only to the social historian, for notwithstanding the predominantly historical perspective which has been taken in this chapter many 'traditional' attitudes to conspicuous economic display still persist in the modern (i.e. present day) world.

Although in more recent years the growth in international communications and the increasing contact between hitherto isolated communities has seen the number of purely traditional societies greatly reduced, they can still be found in many parts of the world. Socially and economically primitive communities, living at subsistence or near-subsistence levels, still exist in Africa, Asia, Australasia and in South America. There are also many feudal societies which masquerade as 'modern' states but which are nevertheless still structured to accommodate ascribed-status minorities supported by a strategic power elite whose own self-interest is to see the status quo maintained.

Finally, and of equal importance, the values of traditional society often still survive within minority sub-cultures in many nations which have without question developed more advanced forms of social organisation and can be considered far more sophisticated in their dominant outlooks and attitudes. These sub-cultures are typically introduced through immigration or have been preserved in relatively underdeveloped regions of otherwise developed, urban economies. Despite their non-dominant position, however, they can still significantly influence, inter alia, many individual intentions and expectations with respect to conspicuous economic display.

The effect of conflicting cultural and sub-cultural influences on conspicuous consumption is of sufficient importance to merit separate consideration at a later stage (q.v.). For the moment, however, it is necessary to move on from traditional societies and to examine the nature and incidence of conspicuous consumption firstly in those societies which have progressed into the phase of rapid population growth and sustained economic expansion and finally in those which have subsequently emerged as the affluent, technologically sophisticated nations of the modern world.

Notes

1   See Firth, R. and Yamey, B.S. (eds), *Capital, Saving and Credit in Peasant Societies,* Allen and Unwin, London, 1964.

2   See Marshall, L., *The Kung Bushmen of the Kalahari Desert,* in Gibbs, J.L. (ed) 'Peoples of Africa', Holt, Rinehart and Winston, New York, 1965. The Kung actively condemned the accumulation of wealth and their gift giving ceremonies were intended to mitigate jealousy, to express friendly interest in community wellbeing and to weave people together in mutual obligation. Again the North American Comanche culture viewed individual wealth display with total indifference. The concept of 'status competition' between individuals was seen as an avoidable social evil (Linton, R., *The Study of Man,* Appleton-Century, New York, 1936, p.453).

3   Linton, R., op.cit.

4   Mair, L., *An Introduction to Social Anthropology*, 2nd edition, Oxford University Press, London, 1972, p.167. In many traditional African communities, for example, rulers had a first claim to rare natural products. Tallensi chiefs had a right to all shea-butter trees in their territory and Ashanti rulers used to claim a third of all gold found by their subjects.

5   The Tanala of Madagascar, for example, believed that the dignity of their privileged elites had to be maintained at all costs and, although these families were expected to spend significantly at such ceremonies as weddings and funerals, it was not acceptable to openly and deliberately display wealth and indulge in ostentatious shows (reference: Linton, R., *The Tanala, a Hill Tribe of Madagascar*, Field Museum of Natural History, vol.XXII, 1933). The Trobriand Islanders of the Western Pacific allowed chiefs sole rights to accumulate large quantities of food—rights which bestowed considerable status. These chiefs were also permitted to transform accumulated food into objects of permanent wealth. These 'vaygua' —objects or tokens of wealth—consisted of several classes of highly valued articles—e.g. axe blades, red shell necklaces and armshells. They were hardly ever put to any real use but were simply highly valued in themselves. Their main function was to be owned as signs of wealth and consequently of status and power and occasionally to change hands as ceremonial gifts. Eighty per cent of the vaygua always remained in the possession of the chiefs and these, plus their food possessions, were the basis of their power, dignity and rank. Thus it was necessary for a chief to secure 'permanent wealth' rather than to indulge in conspicuous expenditure and display in order to secure his status position (reference: Malinowski, B., *The Primitive Economics of the Trobriand Islanders*, in Harding, T.G. and Wallace, B.J. (eds) 'Cultures of the Pacific', Free Press, New York, 1970, pp.51-62.

6   Lannoy, R., *The Speaking Tree—A Study of Indian Culture and Society*, Oxford University Press, London, 1971. See also, Mayer, A.C., *Caste and Kinship in Central India*, Routledge and Kegan Paul, London, 1960.

7   See Lienhardt, G., *Social Anthropology*, 2nd edition, Oxford University Press, London, 1969.

8   In primitive Polynesian society, the Tikopia chiefs concentrated on feasts as their special responsibility, followed by communal distribution of food after the feast itself was over. Through these feasts, the chiefs made use of their command of wealth to maintain position and reputation and set the seal on their status (reference: Firth, R., *Primitive Polynesian Economy*, 2nd edition, Routledge,

London, 1965). The Afikpo Ibo of Nigeria had a 'title society' whose chiefs paid a substantial fee to take the title 'Mmeme' and who could then only secure their prestige by organising and paying for generous public feasts. (Interestingly, by the late 1940s the initiation 'fee' had been waived but the principle of title taking remained. The term 'Mmeme' was redefined to mean 'any socially sanctioned expenditure conferring prestige'—a development which allowed status to be achieved by those with no ascriptive, hereditary rights to social position.) Similarly, the Kpelle of Liberia and the Swazi of Swaziland both awarded status to their paramount chiefs not on the basis of accumulated wealth but by the way in which their wealth was used in the welfare of less fortunate people and the general public interest (references: Ottenberg, P., *The Afikpo Ibo of Eastern Nigeria*; Gibbs, J.L., *The Kpelle of Liberia*; and Kuper, H., *The Swazi of Swaziland* — all in Gibbs, J.L., (ed) 'Peoples of Africa', Holt, Rinehart, Winston, New York, 1965).

9 Sahlius, M.D., *Production, Distribution and Power in a Primitive Society,* in Harding, T.G. and Wallace, B.J. (eds) 'Cultures of the Pacific', Free Press, New York, 1970.

10 Malinowski, B., *Argonauts of the Western Pacific,* 1922.

11 Cipolla, C.M., *Before the Industrial Revolution,* Methuen, London, 1976, Appendix Table A-1.

12 Ibid., p.22.

13 Ibid., p.58.

14 Duby, G., *The Early Growth of the European Economy,* Weidenfield and Nicolson, London, 1973.

15 Cipolla, C.M., op.cit., p.39.

16 Hodgett, G.A.J., *A Social and Economic History of Medieval Europe,* Methuen, London, 1972.

17 Duby, G., op.cit.

18 Ibid., p.232.

19 Heaton, H., *Economic History of Europe,* Harper, New York, 1936, p.359.

20 Finlay, M.I., *The Ancient Economy,* Chatto and Windus, London, 1973, p.129.

21 Ibid., p.139.

22 Cary, M., *A History of Rome,* Macmillan, London, 1947. See also D'Arms J.H., *Romans on the Bay of Naples,* Cambridge, Mass., 1970 and Boethius, A., *The Golden Years of Nero,* Ann Arbor, 1960.

23 Cary, M., op.cit., p.264.

24 Ibid., p.569.

25 By the second century AD there was considerable criticism of explicit 'political' conspicuous expenditure in the form of programmes of amusements for the urban proletariat. Payments made to the increasingly powerful strategic elites were far less obvious. However, these new elites were not slow to imitate the 'nobilitas' (the aristocratic ruling circle) and their own levels of conspicuous consumption increased dramatically. Again, sumptuary laws were introduced or renewed in an attempt to damp down the excesses.

26 See Lannoy, R., op.cit., pp.222-3.

27 Bouglé, C., *Essays on the Caste System,* Cambridge University Press, London, 1971.

28 See Dumont, L., *Contributions to Sociology,* vol.5, October 1961, p.35. Wealthy businessmen (vaishyas) also supported the status quo for, whilst their desire to make money was never lacking, the pursuit of wealth was subordinate to the emotional compulsion to sustain the magico-religious cycle of the 'dharma'—what might be called conspicuous consumption of the potlatch mentality. Ostentatious display for individual status conference was therefore never a significant factor.

29 Maddison, A., *Class Structure and Economic Growth,* Allen and Unwin, London, 1971, p.15.

30 As an example, the Siane of New Guinea allowed 'commoners' to compete for a reputation for generosity with fellow members of the same social grouping but not with members of the social elites. (Salisbury, R.F., *From Stone to Steel,* Cambridge University Press, London, 1962.)

31 See Bouglé, C., op.cit., p.151. Often the entire wealth of a family could be put on display instead of being discreetly hoarded. Bouglé suggests that this competitive display 'leaves almost everyone someone else to despise within the caste system'.

5 Conspicuous consumption in achieving societies

Tradition-directed societies are for the most part 'steady state' economies in which birth and death rates are balanced. Social and economic structures show little if any change over time and the individual's behaviour and ambitions are controlled by his immediate environment and by his position within the community at large. There is a high level of ritual and routine, and lifestyle is predetermined by the group to which a person belongs.

In contrast, developing societies are characterised by far more dynamic economies in which the rate of change of population and of economic development is significantly high. There tends to be considerable accumulation of capital and a reinvestment level which ensures a substantial rate of economic expansion. The individual in such societies is theoretically offered more opportunities for geographic and job mobility and can shape the pattern of his life to a far greater extent than his counterpart born into a rigidly organised, more traditional community.

One of the most significant distinctions between traditional and developing societies is concerned with status and social position. Analysis of primitive and feudal social organisation has shown that status in such societies is overwhelmingly ascribed in that it is awarded on the basis of factors over which the individual has no control—birth, ritual rank, family connections, etc. For the individual in high growth, developing economies, the social and economic flexibility necessary to maintain significant expansion offers an alternative (or additional) reward system in which status can be achieved on the basis of a person's own efforts and merit. Social systems of this latter type have been referred to as 'achieving societies' and offer a distinct contrast with traditional communities in so far as the nature and patterns of conspicuous consumption are concerned.[1]

It would seem reasonable to suppose that the greater opportunities offered for social advancement in achieving societies would lead to a far broader based level of competition for personal prestige and position and that this in turn would encourage the use of conspicuous economic display as a means of securing status gains. High growth economies require that the wealth which tends to accumulate at the top in traditional societies and which is seldom redeployed as investment capital be ploughed back into the economy to sustain economic growth. There needs to be a far wider distribution of income and assets in order to encourage and reward entrepreneurial initiative and hard work. This redistribution of capital and income is paralleled by increasing pressures to award status on the basis of achieved wealth as well as on inherited (ascribed) position.

We could expect to see the motivation for conspicuous consumption considerably increased in achieving societies as status striving individuals recognise the rewards which are offered for displaying accumulated wealth or high income levels. At the same time, the importance of ascribed status should theoretically decline as achieved status becomes established as the dominant motivator and the culturally acceptable standard. The pattern of conspicuous expenditure can be expected to change significantly as many of the rituals of ascriptive societies are made obsolete and replaced by new forms of ostentatious display.

In seeking to compare the theoretical achieving society with its real world counterpart, the experiences of two countries are of particular interest and relevance. Britain was the first society to create a social and economic environment which fostered the first Industrial Revolution and by 1850 was established as the world's first major industrial power. This industrialisation was brought about in a country which was strongly class-conscious and in which, at the time of take off into sustained economic growth, status was clearly ascribed. The United States achieved a similar if somewhat later industrial revolution after 1840 but started from an entirely different base in that it had broken away from, and explicitly rejected, the ascriptive nature of British society and had worked hard to develop a (theoretically) classless achievement-oriented public.

The incidence and pattern of conspicuous consumption in both countries over the 'achieving' years from 1750 onwards is of particular interest. Indeed, what can be considered the 'golden age' of conspicuous consumption is to be found in the American experience from 1860–1914 and it is with the United States that the study is best begun. British social and economic development over the same high growth period can then be examined and contrasted with respect to conspicuous economic display.

The ostentatious excesses of a particular section of American society in the late nineteenth and early twentieth centuries are now a matter of historical record. The fifty years after the Civil War produced levels of conspicuous consumption and conspicuous waste which have rarely been equalled and reflected a mode of behaviour among the rich which prompted Veblen to identify the phenomenon as a major political, economic and social problem of his time.

The excesses of the period were well documented at the time by the American press and the actual level of conspicuous economic display is not in dispute. From 1860 onwards, there was also a 'ratchet effect' in operation as the rich tried to outdo each other in the degree to which they could afford to waste money; the ostentation of the 1870s and 1880s became relatively trivial in comparison to the social spending of the 1890–1910 period.

There can be no doubt that the expenditures in question were conspicuous rather than utilitarian—guests at parties were given one hundred dollar bills with which to light their after-dinner cigars, waterfalls were installed in dining rooms for dinner dances then promptly removed after the entertainment had ended, garden trees were decorated with artificial fruit made of fourteen carat gold. Spending was lavish, always conspicuous and intended solely to achieve social status and recognition.[2]

For much of the period in question, the ostentatious excesses of the very rich created no resentment in those members of society who were relatively deprived in economic terms. To some extent, the conspicuous waste was sustained by a social and economic philosophy which recognised the display of wealth as a legitimate reward for those who had set an example to others. To understand how such a social environment was created and accepted it is necessary to see how America had evolved since the colonial era and her independence and how the achieving society had come into being. . . .

The most striking characteristic of the United States which presents itself in any analysis of the period from 1770 to the Civil War is the magnitude of the impact of religion on its early cultural development. At least six of the colonies that revolted in 1776 had been founded primarily for religious purposes—indeed the initial move to North America from England had occurred during the period of vast religious upheaval in the Old World.[3] Puritan migration to America reached its peak in the 1630s and was followed by a major inflow of Quakers in the 1680s.

The predominance of Protestant beliefs in the 'Colonies' led to a particular emphasis in human affairs—that the welfare of the village or community as a whole should, and must, always take precedence over the welfare of any one particular individual. The settlers were also dedicated to work—an activity they saw as a godly vocation, even as an act of worship—and vehemently rejected conspicuous consumption.

Calvinists, who represented at least fifty per cent of the American people by the time of the Revolution, valued three things above all others—modesty in social and economic affairs, intellect and hard work.

Coming directly from the strong religious beliefs which shaped the cultural norms of the society, the interplay between the Puritan tradition and the Revolutionary ethos produced two themes which were continually stressed in the formation of America's institutions—equality and achievement.[4] The emphasis on equality came not only from deeply held religious conviction but also as a clear revolt against the traditions of the Old World. In addition, the new nation had to prove that it could survive and prosper on its own and achieve substantial progress in social and economic affairs. Consequently, there was a need to convince every citizen that he was as valued as the next man, that he had a very real contribution to make to the prosperity of the United States and that he would be spiritually (n.b.) rewarded in direct proportion to the effort he was prepared to make.

From the Revolution up to the time of the Civil War, Americans were pulled two ways at once. Firstly, there is no doubt of the strong influence of religious values in shaping the early American character. The emphasis on community rather than on individual self-interest was very strong. At the same time, however, there always seems to have been a strong need to seek and establish individual identity and status within a theoretically equal society and conspicuous display was the only means of achieving this, given the relatively classless society in which they lived and the values enshrined in the Constitution. Religious beliefs and social need were therefore often in conflict and this conflict was exacerbated by another key factor—the almost inevitable accumulation of personal wealth.

The greater the individual's commitment—in theory and in practice— to the teachings of the Protestant churches then the more likely he was to become a relatively wealthy man. By applying himself diligently to 'godly' hard work and enterprise, his chances of making a considerable financial surplus over and above his basic needs greatly increased. The churches would and did expect that this surplus be reinvested in new work ventures or in unostentatious consolidation of family comforts but they entirely rejected the possibility that it might be used for conspicuous consumption directed towards individual or family status gains. However, the profit-maker had, according to his religious teachings, simply been rewarded for his correct behaviour and industry and he must often have seen no reason why he should not display rewards to his neighbours and to the community at large. The only means open to him to do so was to display the wealth with which he had been 'blessed'.

This inner conflict between religious orthodoxy and status striving, made worse by the former's ability to supply the wealth with which to indulge the latter—has been a continuing theme in American social history. Prior to 1830, the strength of Protestantism—and in particular the Calvinist and Nonconformist churches—was such that, compared with events after the Civil War, conspicuous consumption was remarkable more by its absence then by its excesses. But pressures had been building up since 1800 which were to change the situation so completely that by the end of the century Veblen was able to draw attention to the massive extravagances of the 'Gilded Age'.[5]

From 1800 onwards there was a highly significant rise in achievement motivation in the American social character—a rise reflected in literature and in writings throughout the nineteenth century. As in Britain prior to the Industrial Revolution, this rise in achievement level proceded the take off into complete industrialisation after 1870. But it also required that the emphasis shifted from community interest to the individual pursuit of wealth as a worthy aim in itself.

McClelland has shown that the mean frequency of achievement imagery increased by a factor of five between the years 1800—1890 in the United States.[6] This highly significant change in social attitudes reflected a fundamental change in the doctrine of 'self-help' which had traditionally argued that any individual could and should achieve worldly success simply through hard work. The seventeenth and eighteenth century forms of the doctrine were entirely theological and stipulated that God wanted man to work hard and prosper in his chosen vocation, but after 1800 self-help began to detach itself from its religious moorings and ever since has been secular in its implications. It is important at this stage to understand how and why this fundamental change in values came about. . . .

Prior to the Civil War, there was an aristocracy of sorts in the theoretically 'classless' United States. There is considerable evidence to show that the Anglophilia of the colonial plutocracy had passed virtually intact to their feudal successors in power and thence to the beneficiaries of second and third generation wealth in Boston, New York and Philadelphia.[7] The gentry of 1800—1850 were the merchants of longstanding and, perhaps more importantly, the professional classes. 'Society' was directed by lawyers, physicians and professors who, in effect, formed a class rather than a profession and 'acted not as individuals but as though they were clergymen and each profession was a church'.[8]

The ascendancy of the traditional aristocracy was being constantly eroded after 1800—slowly at first but with an increasing momentum. A new elite born out of the prosperity of industry and commerce was beginning to emerge and prosper. The rise of the private corporation after 1840 helped consolidate the wealth and position of the growing number of successful men of business who were introducing an industrial revolution to the United States. The professional men who had inherited their positions from the colonial era and who had been strong supporters of the Protestant work ethic and of theological values closely identified with dissenting beliefs managed to retain their status and position until the Civil War but could not survive the peace. In the post war period all was changed. The building of great industrial plant, the construction of the railroads, the emergence of the corporation as the dominant form of enterprise, transformed the old society and revolutionised the distribution of power and prestige.[9]

The decline of inherited colonial power and status and the emergence of an industrial elite was reflected in a break from the old theological interpretation of the work ethic and the establishment of a new definition of self-help which lent itself more easily to the changing social and economic realities of the time and which in effect paved the way for the conspicuous economic excesses which were to become so evident in the Gilded Age and through to the First World War.

The new United States needed a high rate of economic growth but if this growth was to be achieved there had to be a real incentive for entrepreneurs to invest time and money in industrial and commercial expansion.[10] The traditional Puritan view had always been to promote such ambitions by promising a rich and happy existence in the next life but it was becoming increasingly difficult to motivate young men on the basis of such an intangible reward system. For business to prosper, the emphasis had to shift from the community to individual welfare and had to establish the respectability of seeking conspicuous rewards in this life rather than in the next.

The process of re-education was helped in two important ways. Firstly, the accumulation of wealth and the suppression of conspicuous display under the 'old' system had created a climate in which any re-interpretation in favour of dis-saving and the ostentatious enjoyment of such wealth was bound to flourish. Secondly, the Protestant church had become 'respectable' and institutionalised and was less ready to move strongly against a reinterpretation of the work ethic which did not directly attack the established churches.

The changing value system found expression in American literature from the 1830s onwards. Hawthorne (1832), Washington Irving (1836) and Ralph Waldo Emerson (1841) were among the many writers who began the movement towards individualism and the pursuit of wealth for its own sake. Very few chose to oppose them, although Thoreau (1854) denounced the philosophy of 'getting on' and the commercialism which 'has atrophied the creative and spiritual lives of my countrymen'.[11]

After the Civil War, the new philosophy was clearly established and had itself become a part of the American character. As the Gilded Age began, the doctrine of self-help penetrated, in some guise, every major activity and America witnessed the rise and apotheosis of the successful businessman. Between 1860 and the end of the century, American writings frequently restated the 'new religion'.[12] Following the publication of Samuel Smiles' *Self-Help* in 1859, the cult of the self-made man became an essential part of American social thought and prospered for half a century or more.[13]

The new climate created by the self-help doctrine after the Civil War prepared the ground for the affluent business community to gain enormously in stature and status and to put down a social challenge to the traditional elite. Before 1860 there had been many successful businessmen who had accumulated substantial wealth but at that time they had not seen fit to engage in conspicuous competition with the old aristocracy. In a sense, they still 'knew their place' and did not seek to challenge for social ascendancy:

> In the 1840s and early 1850s, these new plutocrats had nasty manners and their business would have made anyone blush. Yet there was one thing to be said for them. They did not, like their successors in plutocracy, bedizen their women and bedazzle the public with ostentatious luxury. Their most lavish gestures had some social value. Sizeable sums went to institutions of learning—the Astors, for example, gave four hundred thousand dollars to set up the Astor Library.[14]

It was the ostentation not of the 1840—1860 business elite but of their heirs which ultimately gave rise to talk of the Astor's excesses and the absurdities of Ward McAllister's list of four hundred 'exclusively eligible families'. But the foundations for the conspicuous consumption of the 1880—1910 period were the fortunes made between 1840 and 1870—fortunes which multiplied as the American 'Industrial Revolution' was established and brought ever increasing wealth to the business community.

The years after 1860 saw the very rich use their wealth in a way which totally broke with tradition. They sought to gain in social ranking, position and prestige by riding on the back of the self-help philosophy and displaying the massive wealth and financial strength they enjoyed. The competition between old and new 'aristocracies' became so intense that the period after 1880 has been called 'the era of the status revolution'.[15]

It is ironic that the status revolutionaries who undertook such significant conspicuous consumption to secure status gains could claim no real support from the self-help doctrine which argued that men should enjoy rewards and privileges according to their own effort. In truth, the great business leaders and conspicuous consumers of the Gilded Age were typically men who started from comfortable and privileged beginnings in life and who had never had to work to secure the basic wealth on which their fortunes were built. It was their fathers and grandfathers who had been rewarded for effort but who had either saved or reinvested their fortunes or used them for socially (and religiously) approved philanthropic expenditures.[16] The self-help doctrine was so useful in justifying the extravagances of their successors, however, that a process of 'myth-making' took place after 1860—a process encouraged by the new generation—which sought to establish that the conspicuous consumers had come from poverty to riches by dint of hard work, perseverance and industrial know-how.[17]

The concentration of wealth after 1860 ensured that the privileged business elite had all the necessary resources to wage the status war to the death. During the 1840s there were probably no more than twenty millionaires in the entire country but by 1910 there were more than twenty millionaires sitting in the United States Senate.[18] In 1891 it was estimated that there were 120 men in the United States each of whom was worth over ten million dollars.[19] In 1892, the New York Tribune published a list of 4,047 reputed millionaires and the Census Bureau looked at concentration of wealth and estimated that 9 per cent of the families of the nation owned 71 per cent of the wealth. And, in addition to the significant rise in wealth concentrations, the 'soft' tax system and the general economic climate created by the take off into industrialisation after 1870 both served to ensure that accumulated wealth was, in effect, readily available as personal spending money.

The inordinately high levels of conspicuous consumption which were in evidence particularly after 1880 have already been commented upon. Most expenditures of this type were so 'conspicuous' that their direct utility was minimal or zero, and there can be no doubt that status goals were the prime movers behind such ostentatious economic display. The rich were, in effect, trying to establish a code of behaviour in which belonging to 'Society' was a function of money rather than of inherited position or breeding. At Mrs Astor's dinner parties 'dowagers of impeccable ancestry had been observed to weep when denied a place on the dais'.[20] A new social order was in process of manufacture in which wealth was the only criterion for membership.

The status revolution of the Gilded Age is well documented, particularly as the press took considerable pains to report the latest conspicuous excesses of the 'new aristocracy' to their readers who appeared to have an insatiable appetite for such affairs. However, the revolution was never easy. There had always been a considerable opposition to the social aspirations of the newly rich. Firstly, the old colonial elite who saw their position of privilege under attack fought long and hard to protect their social position. They counterattacked by invoking hereditary privilege and insisted that birth and breeding were the only real considerations in any system of social ranking. In essence, they were claiming that ascribed status necessarily took precedence over achieved status. This reassertion of traditional values was accompanied by the creation of genealogy-minded societies which conspicuously barred the rich from membership unless they could produce tangible evidence of ascribed position and prestige. Of 105 patriotic orders founded between 1783 and 1900, 34 originated before 1870 and 71 between 1870 and 1900.[21] Between 1875 and 1894 were founded the Sons of the Revolution, Sons of the American Revolution, the Daughters of the American Revolution, the Colonial Dames of America and the Society of Mayfair Descendants.[22] The societies actively discriminated against—and looked down upon—the 'parvenu' who could show no inherited pedigree, and their campaign was successful enough to ensure that many of the 'new men' sought to marry into the old gentry in order to bring a necessary ascribed status into their families.

The second attack on the new social order came from a group of writers and intellectuals who had never accepted the reinterpretation of self-help as anything more than a weakening of traditional morality and values. Thoreau was perhaps the first to question the new philosophy but he was followed by others who pursued the same theme. In the Gilded Age, Mark Twain and Charles Warner satirised the cult of the self-made man in America by creating Colonel Beriah Sellers (1873). After 1880, a growing number of novelists began to cast doubts on the cult of individualism. The realities of poverty and cruelty in rural America were exposed.[23] Grim reviews of urban poverty were also presented.[24] And there was another interpretation put forward to explain the vast inequalities of wealth which arose in the late nineteenth century and early twentieth centuries—i.e. that the great fortunes enjoyed by the new industrial barons reflected massive deprivation at the other end of the social scale. In 1890, 11 million of America's 12.5 million families lived on an average of only $380 per year, and statistics such as these led to an increasing realisation that the inequalities prompted by the self-help philosophy could and did create what to many observers was an unfair and unjust society. Self-help proponents could reply, of course, that financial success built on hard work was God-given and that the solution to poverty lay fairly and squarely in the hands of the poor themselves.

There is little doubt that until 1890, and despite the growing criticism, the apostles of self-help were on balance winning the philosophical and moral battle and continued to attract thousands of devotees. However, after that year the spokesmen for the new order became markedly more defensive in their writings and utterances as their antagonists grew in numbers and in strength. Not all industrialists were themselves convinced that the accumulation of wealth merited conspicuous behaviour of a wasteful, ostentatious nature. Andrew Carnegie—one of the outstandingly successful businessmen of the period—wrote an essay on 'Wealth' in 1889 in which he supported self-help as a legitimate mechanism for wealth creation but condemned the ostentatious display which so often accompanied it:

This, then, is held to be the duty of the man of wealth: First, to set an example of modest unostentatious living, shunning

display or extravagance; to provide moderately for the legitimate wants of those dependent upon him; and after doing so
to consider all surplus revenues which come to him simply as
trust funds, which he is called upon to administer in the
manner which, in his judgement, is best calculated to produce
the most beneficial results for the community.

And again:

What is modest unostentatious living: what is the test of
extravagance?. . . . Public sentiment is quick to know and to
feel what offends (good taste). . . Whatever makes one conspicuous offends the canon. If any family be chiefly known
for display, for extravagance at home, table, equipage, for
enormous sums ostentatiously spent in any form upon itself—
if these be its chief distinctions, we have no difficulty in
estimating its nature on culture. . . . The community will
surely judge and its judgements will not often be wrong.[25]

Notwithstanding the exhortations of Carnegie and a few other self-
made men of wealth, conspicuous consumption itself continued on a
grand scale throughout the 1890s and well into the twentieth century.
The press continued to report on the excesses and extravagances of
'Society' throughout the period. Life under pioneer conditions of earlier
times may have taught people how to work rather than how to spend
but the late nineteenth century newly rich turned to conspicuous display
with the same fierce energy. Society life in the great cities was characterised by wasteful, ostentatious expenditure which achieved astonishing
levels as the rich attempted to make themselves socially exclusive and
elite. In essence the twin aristocracies of birth and wealth were fighting
a prolonged battle for ascendancy which did not subside until the First
World War.

The fastest rate of growth in ostentatious economic display was
probably recorded in the period 1890–1910, due in no small part to
the fact that the money (and spending) needed to be considered 'super
rich' began to grow every year at a faster and faster rate.[26] By the turn
of the century, ideas as to money values—and as to conspicuous consumption—moved to accommodate the hundreds of millions of dollars
that Carnegie and other major industrialists were then said to be worth.
In the early 1900s 'billionaires' arrived on the scene and the ratchet
effect was again in evidence as more and more money was spent to buy
a place on the social register.[27]

The exponential growth of conspicuous consumption after 1890 was
responsible for its eventual decline. The amounts being spent in seeking
to secure social position became so great that the public reacted and
began to turn against the big spenders of the day. By the early 1900s
the number of Americans disenchanted by the spectacle of the 'idle rich'

had grown much greater and their disapproval and displeasure had deepened. The press began to take a significantly different attitude to the behaviour and high spending of the rich and the 'Muckraker' era of journalism came into vogue as newspaper editors sensed a changing attitude on the part of the general public to the financial excesses of the status seekers. Instead of commenting with considerable deference and admiration on the social antics of the rich, a sharp note of disapproval was evident in much of the reporting after the turn of the century. There was undoubtedly a growing feeling throughout the United States that the self-help philosophy which had prospered since 1860 was producing a social and economic structure which was increasingly unacceptable to Americans in general.

The new social climate was in effect reflecting a changing political mood which was directly opposed to conspicuous expenditure and consumption. During the first years of the twentieth century, progressivism grew and flourished as a philosophy which argued that the more able in society should look after the less able and that community welfare should be actively encouraged by the political and social system. In many ways, this new doctrine was a return to the 'traditional' Protestant values which had been modified in the years of great industrial growth to accommodate the social aspirations of the new rich. It became increasingly attractive after 1900 and led to demands that the vast profits of the industrial community be channelled into the public purse rather than dissipated in acts of often outrageous conspicuous economic display. Programmes of action were put forward for more and better education, for attacks on poverty, for reform of moral values and for the prevention and cure of disease.[28] Such programmes clearly needed financing on a hitherto unknown scale and activists linked such proposals with strong attacks on the current 'squandering' of the economic surplus of the nation.

The last recognisable statement in favour of Gilded Age self-help appeared in 1901, after which proponents of individual achievement—in its pure form—became increasingly quiet and defensive.[29] The new religion argued that the nation at large had a responsibility to lower the individual's expectations of rising to great wealth and to ensure that success came to be measured more in terms of sound character and good deeds. Although conspicuous consumption remained at very high levels up to the First World War and the rich tried as hard as they could to secure their wealth based privileges, the change in mood was becoming more and more evident. Walter Weyl, one of the intellectual spokesmen for progressivism, not only argued in favour of public redistribution of wealth but pointed out that the whole process of competitive conspicuous consumption was necessarily socially divisive:

By setting the pace for a frantic competitive consumption, our

77

infinite gradations in wealth (with which gradations the plutocracy is inevitably associated) increase the general social friction and produce an acute social irritation. We are developing a new type of destitutes—the automobileless, the yachtless, the Newport cottageless. The subtlest of luxuries become necessities, and their loss is bitterly resented. The discontent of today reaches very high in the social scale.[30]

The First World War effectively ended the remarkable excesses of conspicuous consumption which had been in evidence in the United States certainly since 1880. In the post war years it was no longer socially or politically possible to indulge in ostentatious display to the outrageous levels which had been observed in earlier years. Economic wealth was nevertheless still concentrated in the hands of a relatively small industrially based elite, as a succession of administrations (Wilson, Coolidge, Harding) were clearly sympathetic to big business and looked to the top industrialists of the day for political and financial support. However, the Great Depression of 1929–1933 destroyed much of the industrial and personal wealth of the country and the election of Roosevelt in 1932—a politician whose New Deal required that the power of the industrial barons be broken—ensured that the era of conspicuous consumption in its Gilded Age form had come to an end.

In the period after 1920, the incidence of conspicuous consumption undertaken to achieve new status gains had been declining. Overt personal display of wealth was rapidly becoming a social liability rather than a means to improve position and prestige. However, the motivation for such economic behaviour was also far less strong and the conspicuous expenditure levels of the 1880–1915 period would not have been maintained after the war irrespective of the new social, political and economic order. This was simply due to the fact that conspicuous consumption had in fact already secured a considerable status gain for the industrialists who had seen their fortunes multiply during the take off period into industrialisation and sustained economic growth. After 1920, the new problem was one of status consolidation rather than status achievement and this saw a significant shift in the conspicuous expenditure patterns of the rich away from personal indulgence and towards philanthropic projects.

Conspicuous philanthropy was no new development. The early industrialists who had built fortunes in the 1840s and 1850s had concentrated their economic wealth on instituting schemes of charity and public works. Later, Andrew Carnegie—who never condoned the excess consumption of his contemporaries—had pioneered the grand philanthropic gesture and between 1902 and 1911 had created the Carnegie Institute, the Carnegie Corporation and other charitable trusts.[31] The Rockefeller family had also been conspicuous only by their involvement with longer term projects for social improvement. For the majority of other industrialists of the late nineteenth and early twentieth centuries, public works came a poor second to the ostentatious display and waste of vast wealth, but after the First World War this newly established social elite turned to philanthropic works as an ideal vehicle for consolidating their newly won social rank.

High expenditure on public projects and social assets fitted well with the political and social doctrines of progressivism and had a respectability which the excesses of the Gilded Age never achieved. The rich therefore turned to them with enthusiasm: by 1920 a hundred personally financed foundations, agencies and charitable trusts had been established but by 1931 the number had risen to in excess of 350. The wheel had turned full circle and the pattern of conspicuous expenditure mirrored that of the pre-Civil War era; once again community came before self and the undiluted doctrine of individualism ceased to dominate social and economic activity.

With the benefit of hindsight, the Gilded Age preoccupation with individual enterprise and its acceptance of high levels of status-directed conspicuous consumption have been roundly condemned by intellectuals, modern historians and social theorists. The self-help philosophy is considered to have failed in that, whilst everyone willing to work hard was theoretically supposed to succeed, the fundamental inequalities of human beings meant that certain more fortunate individuals achieved far greater rewards than those who found it difficult to raise their work rate or develop any entrepreneurial talents. This basic 'innate' inequality was made worse by the fact that all 'competitors' in the race did not start with the same social and economic advantages—indeed, substantial evidence exists to show that the successful few were almost always inordinately privileged and rich before they amassed their own fortunes.

Notwithstanding the distaste with which the ostentatious excesses of the era of the status revolution have been received, there can at the same time be little doubt that, overall, the objectives of the conspicuous consumers were largely achieved. A cursory glance at the names which made the headlines at that time will confirm that the majority of the attempts to establish status gains through the overt consumption of wealth were successful. The descendants of many Gilded Age conspicuous consumers are today firmly located in the national 'social register' and are establishment figures in their own right. Whilst it is clearly impossible to show the precise extent to which ostentatious display contributed to past status gains, conspicuous consumption—linked to the self-help philosophy—was certainly a major factor in securing prestige and recognition.

The success of conspicuous consumers was in no small part due to the recognition that Americans of all classes—with the possible exception of the old East Coast 'aristocracy'—have always given to wealth and to the wealthy. As early as 1830, many visitors to the United States were struck by the extent to which American workers adopted a spendthrift pattern of consumption whenever possible and attempted to imitate higher class lifestyles.[32] A report published in 1837 commented:

> The population of the United States is beyond that of other countries an anxious one. All classes are either striving after wealth or endeavouring to keep up its appearance. From the principle of imitation which is implanted in all of us, sharpened perhaps by the existing equality of conditions, the poor follow as closely as they are able the habits and manners of living of the rich.[33]

Wealth and the privileges that go with it have never been greatly resented in the United States but have often stimulated those less fortunate to emulate the successful. Wealthy families have in consequence enjoyed a considerable status and prestige which has often been absent in other societies. Paradoxically, the very great emphasis placed on equality as a fundamental of American society may have produced a great respect for money and for wealth which can still be observed today. Precisely as a result of the stress laid on the need for equality of treatment and of opportunity, Americans were (and are) often more status conscious than those who lived in the more aristocratic societies of Europe.[34] Many observers have pointed out that the preoccupation with ensuring that all men are equal, and the lack of a clear deference structure linked to a legitimate aristocratic tradition in which the propriety of social rankings are unquestioned, forced Americans to actually stress status, background and symbolism.

Because individuals were given no clear social 'frame of reference' within which they could locate themselves and others, they increasingly felt the need to create or invent one. This need to manufacture a social ranking system persisted throughout the 'achieving society' period which certainly endured to 1940. As late as 1943, the following observations could be made:

> America is today a society, which, despite all efforts of school, advertising, clubs and the rest makes the creation of effective social barriers difficult and their maintenance a perpetually repeated task. American social fences have to be continually repaired; in England they are like wild hedges, they grow if left alone.[35]

and. . . .

> It is only an apparent contradiction in terms to assert that the fundamental democratic and egalitarian character of American life is demonstrated by the ingenuity and persistence shown in inventing marks of difference and symbols of

superiority. In a truly class-conscious and caste-dominated society, the marks of difference are universally recognised even if resented. In America, they must be stressed or they might easily be forgotten, and they must be added to, as the old standards of distinction cease to serve their purpose. Apart from the simple economic criterion of conspicuous display, there are no generally accepted marks of social difference in America.[36]

On American evidence alone, conspicuous consumption would seem to be a significant—perhaps even a necessary—factor in sustaining high growth achieving societies but to what extent can the American pattern of conspicuous economic display be considered typical? Whilst rates of population growth and of industrial development were broadly similar to those which have been found in other countries at their corresponding stages of economic growth, it is nevertheless possible that the special conditions which obtained in the United States during the Gilded Age were such that the resultant pattern of conspicuous consumption was entirely atypical.

In order to properly assess the degree to which the American experience may be generalised, it is helpful to compare and contrast it with that of a culturally 'sympathetic' community which has undergone a similar pattern of social and economic development over a comparable period of time. To this end, the experience of Britain from 1700 to 1940 offers possibly the best yardstick against which to judge the United States evidence and incidence of conspicuous consumption.[37]

On practical grounds, Britain offers a lucrative field of study in that it provides the longest and most intensively studied record of early economic and industrial growth.[38] The country was at the centre of an industrial revolution which ushered in the modern era of sustained industrialisation and its society came under many of the stresses and strains which were experienced at a later time in the United States.

The social and economic development of Britain as an achieving society, and in particular the associated record of conspicuous consumption, are best examined in two distinct parts—firstly, the period 1700–1840 and secondly the Victorian and Edwardian eras leading through the First World War to 1940. Looking at the lead-in to the earlier period, from Tudor times onwards there was developing a clear shift away from the gross inequalities of wealth distribution associated with the political power of feudal aristocracies and towards an economic structure which increasingly enabled more and more people to enjoy a relatively high level of wealth and income. This movement was to a large extent due to the rise in power and status of the gentry and landowners at the expense of the traditional aristocracy.

Peers of the Tudor period still had considerable wealth but aristocratic power based on old feudal loyalties and privileges was in slow decline as the upper gentry began to emerge:

> It is not difficult to produce evidence of conspicuous extravagance among the peers. They spent vast sums on building their great houses and the style of these became more extravagant in the course of the sixteenth century. Heavy expenditure on clothes was another item, and not content with fabulous ostentation in life, some peers were magnificent in death also. As an example, the Earl of Leicester's funeral cost £3,000 at 1561 prices. However, social conservatism began to fall as the acquisition of wealth by the landed gentry led to quite speedy recognition, in the second generation if not the first. Personal distinction, based on wealth, could increasingly offset lowly birth. Thus although Tudor society was undoubtedly class conscious, an able man could climb socially a good way without meeting serious obstacles, and wealth acquired respectability within a generation.[39]

Throughout the seventeenth century, the shift of economic and social power away from the traditional aristocracies and towards the newly rich upper gentry and landowners continued. This trend was reinforced and acknowledged by the ennobling of the new country-based elite from Elizabethan times onwards and the gradual creation of a 'new' aristocracy—a process which continued through the Stuart and Cromwellian period and which received added impetus in the eighteenth century under the stimulus of the Georges and the Agrarian Revolution which laid even greater emphasis on the contribution of the great country estates to the agricultural prosperity of the country at large. By the late eighteenth century, the decline of the Old Guard and the major shift of wealth and influence to the new landed gentry had been consolidated.[40]

This change in social and economic relationships brought with it a parallel change in the ability and desire of privileged individuals to conspicuously consume. As landowners grew wealthier, embellishments to their houses were added—often of a superfluous and paltry kind. The vogue for the 'Gothic' encouraged the building of ostentatious homes and residences and it became a popular pastime with the local gentry and travellers to visit great houses and view their splendours.[41]

The riches enjoyed by the English landed gentry from 1700 to c.1820 were perhaps greater than any class had hitherto enjoyed. The wealth—and the conspicuous consumption that went with it—was spent on mansions, furniture and servants. Country families conspicuously visited and consumed in various fashionable resorts throughout the country. Almost everything the rich did served the ends of style. Above all, it was an era of building—Gothic lodges, Ionic arches and Corinthian pillars. By July 1813 the United States, then at war with Britain, was unable to borrow as much money as one particular nobleman could raise on his private credit.[42] And such was the general respect for wealth that Englishmen clearly felt reluctant to entrust political power to any man who did not have it. By 1815 four-fifths of the House of Commons and almost the entire hereditary personnel of the House of Lords were landowners.[43]

Eighteenth and early nineteenth century levels of conspicuous consumption were significantly high because at that time the position of the rich 'seemed as unalterable as the great palaces which housed them'.[44] The gentry, building their lives on the massive deference and respect paid to them by all people and classes, were able to indulge in levels of wasteful expenditure which are allowed only to those who feel no threat from those who observe them. The rich had become almost too rich; to live expensive and elegant lives had become the end of existence by 1820. The splendours and excesses of Regency society must have seemed eternal to the men and women of the time and to rich and poor alike the order of society appeared to be unchangeable.

The poor were as poor as the rich were rich. The early years of the Industrial Revolution after 1750 did not dramatically shift the rural-urban balance but where industrialisation did take place the workers were generally paid and housed at subsistence level and given little or no opportunity to emulate the conspicuous economic behaviour of the country landowners. The rural workers were similarly deprived and could not hope to achieve any real level of material prosperity. There can have been few periods in English history in which the differences in income and wealth between rich and poor were so marked and seemed to be so permanent.

Notwithstanding the overwhelming inequality of income and wealth distribution, observers of the time were often convinced that all Britons were increasingly becoming martyrs to display.[45] It was believed elsewhere in Europe that the dominant desire of all classes in Britain—irrespective of financial standing—was to 'cut a dash':

> The necessity for all people, not merely the real necessaries and comforts of life but the means of living in style, a certain inveterate habit of luxury, inexorable vanity, answer in England the same purpose as the conscription in France, and the fondest mother thinks as little of resisting the one as the other.[46]

The extravagant lifestyles of the rich had been financed after 1800 primarily by British agriculture to which more than two decades of war with France (1793—1815) had brought an artificial prosperity. However, the excesses of the Regency did not last. Agriculture suffered badly under a post war deflation which led directly into a sustained fall in farm prices lasting until 1849. Although there was continual demand that agriculture must find the money to pay for the luxurious and expensive tastes of the landowning classes, the general depression following the end of the Napoleonic wars had increased the levels of poverty not only for the unskilled but for the skilled industrial worker and increasing pressure for political reform was built up throughout the 1820s. This pressure culminated in the 1832 Reform Bill which effectively set the scene for a radical change in society by breaking the landed gentry's monopoly of politics and thus of economic management.

The changing climate after 1820 ensured that the great ostentation of the Regency was followed by a less 'conspicuous' period in which far reaching political, economic and social reforms were much in evidence and were laying the basis for the new industrial and predominantly middle class Victorian era. By the time Victoria came to the throne, the power of the landed gentry—although still great—was in clear decline.

In essence, the excesses of conspicuous consumption which built up after 1700 and reached a peak in the early nineteenth century were made possible because the landowners had not only the wealth (i.e. the ability) to behave ostentatiously but also enjoyed a political power and a social position which was absolute. The deference shown by one class for another (superior) one was pervasive and unquestioned. Consequently—as with early forms of feudal society—there was no social or political risk associated with economic self-indulgence and the levels of expenditure grew accordingly. The major distinction between the two social structures lay only in the fact that whilst aristocratic status in feudal times was ascribed and typically derived from inherited position and privilege, the eighteenth century nobility had achieved status through the ownership and exploitation of land and had become the new strategic elite.

In seeking to explain the consumption behaviour of the eighteenth century elites it is instructive to examine the extent to which individuals in general were motivated to achieve status from the Tudor period onwards. In his comprehensive analysis of achieving societies both past and present, McClelland identified a pattern of achievement motivation which perhaps helps to explain the nature and incidence of conspicuous consumption over the years in question. The first period examined, centred on the years 1500 to 1600, showed a pattern of high achievement stimuli which had resulted from the status opportunities offered by the slow decline of the 'old' aristocracy—a decline which created the vacuum subsequently filled by the landed gentry. This was followed by a period of significant stagnation and a marked lack of achievement stimuli extending from 1600 to 1700. Finally, from 1700 onwards, achievement levels built up dramatically and showed a phenomenal rise throughout the century.[47]

There was also a very close connection established between high achievement motivation and the rise of Protestantism. The increase in achievement indicators after 1700 ran parallel to a Protestant revival. 1729 saw the foundation of the nonconformist Methodist Church and the dissenting bodies were gaining in strength and influence throughout the eighteenth century. After 1800, when Protestantism became less active but increasingly 'respectable', achievement motivators fell significantly.[48]

The high achievement motivation which persisted throughout the eighteenth century appears to have stimulated the correspondingly high levels of ostentatious economic display already referred to, although conspicuous consumption tended to reach its highest levels after achievement stimuli had 'peaked'. However, these high achievement scores and conspicuous consumption levels do not themselves correlate with periods of high economic growth. In the eighteenth century, national income per capita was showing a steady but slow rise up to 1770 and even a slight decline after 1770 in the early years of the Industrial Revolution proper. The peak of ostentatious living and conspicuous display in the Regency period coincided with a period of significant national income per capita decline.[49] Broadly speaking, high achieved status motivators and conspicuous expenditure levels were consistently 'out of phase' with economic growth—measured in national income per capita terms—from 1700 to 1820.

McClelland's work was primarily concerned with testing the hypothesis that periods of high achievement motivation tend to precede times of high economic growth. He was successful in 'fitting' economic growth (measured in trade volume terms) to high achievement indicators if a fifty year lag was allowed between the two.[50] In so far as the present study is concerned, the evidence seems to support the proposition that, in achieved status societies, conspicuous economic behaviour is most in evidence not during periods of initial wealth accumulation resulting from high levels of economic activity but rather in the post growth period when achieved status is being established and consolidated through the ostentatious display of acquired wealth.

If conspicuous consumption was at its highest when the economic elites had consolidated their position and were at their most secure, what motivations lay behind their ostentatious behaviour? The principal incentive seems to have been to secure status gains at the expense of economic and social equals—i.e. the conspicuous consumption at the top of the social pyramid appears to have been 'horizontal' in that it represented status competition within a particular class. However, a further motivation may well have been 'vertical' in that, starting from a position of high relative economic and political strength, conspicuous expenditure could serve to reinforce the status quo with those of less exalted social rank. High levels of spending by the rich and powerful could serve to emphasise to those less fortunate how great was the economic gap between the classes. Seen from a position of near absolute authority and power, such a strategy could clearly be attractive but if conspicuous consumption was undertaken for such reasons, then it has to be seen as a partly political rather than an exclusively social act. One positive side effect of the vertical reinforcement of achieved status was that it gave a rationale to the upper gentry's competitive ostentatious display. They could convince themselves—if not others—that excessive expenditure and waste was necessary at higher levels of society to secure the existing (and by implication satisfactory) social, economic and political order.

Throughout the eighteenth century there had been a steady rise in the numbers and importance of a 'middle class'—traders and businessmen who were prospering and who were increasingly able to accumulate a respectable degree of wealth. The growth of this class corresponded with the increase in achievement indicators already mentioned but it is interesting to note that the middle class propensity to conspicuously consume was never a threat or challenge to the landowning strategic elite. The voluntary control—even rejection—of ostentatious display can be attributed in part to their often strict adherence to the Protestant faith which effectively condemned overt consumption as being self-glorifying. When the middle classes did indulge in conspicuous behaviour, moreover, it was only to 'copy' the ostentatious display of the gentry for whom they clearly had the greatest respect and admiration. As already mentioned, the landowning elite enjoyed a personal prestige and standing up to 1820 which went virtually unchallenged. Their political and social position appeared totally secure, both to themselves and to others. In such circumstances, the emergent middle class simply emulated the behaviour of their acknowledged superiors, although it is possible that such emulation was intended in part as a means to secure vertical status gains in that the established elite would perhaps be willing to accept imitation as an acceptable form of flattery which could be socially rewarded.[51]

In the Victorian years after 1840 and through the Edwardian era to 1914, the single most striking development was the emergence of the middle class as the dominant influence on political, social and economic affairs. The Industrial Revolution had given the opportunity of relative wealth and prosperity to many thousands who in earlier years could have entertained no hopes of making significant social or economic advances. As standards of living improved for the middle classes, there was also a clear 'trickle down' effect to the poor and deprived whose own expectations changed and who were no longer entirely passive in seeking social and political change.

Although the period after 1840 was one of considerable reform, the pattern of conspicuous consumption appears to have changed remarkably little. Throughout the Victorian and Edwardian years, the aristocracy fought a rearguard battle to maintain their privileges. They slowly conceded ground in politics and economics but were most successful in retaining their hold on matters of social prestige.[52] Their success in this area was due to many factors which, taken together, produced a considerable resistance to radical changes in power and social privilege of the sort which took place at approximately the same time in the United States.

The period 1850–1875 was a time of massive industrial build-up and strength in England and generated a level of wealth creation sufficient to satisfy many if not all of the financial aspirations of those whose political power had been increasing since the reform period of 1820–1850. It was only after 1875 and the arrival of the Great Depression which lasted more or less until the end of the century that the economic pressures on the traditionally privileged were strong enough to force greater changes in social and economic organisation. However, the British middle and working classes never really lost their deference and respect for their historical 'betters' and sought to emulate rather than replace them. This deference was to be observed at all levels on the social ladder but more particularly within the various middle class ranks. Whilst the working classes were more likely to consume leisure and comfort with discretionary income (if any), the lower middle class aspired to imitate upper middle class lifestyles. The middle class proper, however, were concerned for the most part not with challenging the upper classes but with consolidating and preserving the 'gap' between themselves and the classes below them from which most often they themselves had sprung. This combination of deference to existing elites and competition for status within the broad middle class itself left the basic hierarchy of status and privilege largely unchallenged and the inherent superiority of the upper classes unchanged.

So limited were the changes in the first half of the Victorian era that the period 1850-1870 has been referred to as the 'Age of Equipoise'.[53] The topmost strata of the British hierarchy—i.e. the hereditary nobility and country gentry—can not be considered to have been seriously challenged. After the 'quieter' years of conspicuous display in the 1830 to 1850 reform period—an inevitable reaction to the Regency excesses which had triggered much of the political radicalism and revolt of the 1830s and 1840s—upper class conspicuous consumption was again built up to substantial levels with the most extravagance being reflected in magnificent properties and country houses. During the 1830–1850 period a part of the newly affluent middle class did for a time see themselves as fighting a social battle with the traditional elite but by the 1850s they had clearly lost and had conceded defeat.[54] The ostentatious lifestyles and social prestige of the upper classes were not under serious threat throughout the period.

The situation changed noticeably after 1875 as the country moved into relative industrial and agricultural depression and it was in the period following the general economic collapse that it became clear to the landed aristocracy that the traditional social and economic order could not survive. The first indication of the changing forces at work in late Victorian times was the decreasing significance of the ownership of great tracts of land as the primary source of combined wealth and social status.[55] The agricultural disasters of 1882 and 1897 were to destroy much of the financial base of the rural gentry. Again, the political scene was changing more rapidly and trade unions became established and adopted increasingly militant stances against the inequalities of income distribution and of lifestyle. The size and depth of the recession meant that expectations and aspirations which had been building up throughout the century were far more difficult to fulfil.

The landed aristocracy reacted to these new pressures carefully and astutely. The decline of agriculture and the falling royalties from urban and suburban land development had eroded their financial security. The new industrialists were now rapidly becoming the new rich. Consequently, the establishment moved its money into collaborative industrial enterprises and joined the boards of many important companies (helped in this by the social prestige industrialists believed to come from having titled directors in their boardrooms). By effectively forging an alliance with the new industrialists who, by and large, had prospered throughout Victorian times, the wealth and privileges of the old elite were restored and even strengthened. An observer of the time commented:

> The aristocratic principle is still paramount, forms the foundation of our social structure and has been strengthened and extended in its operation by the plutocratic element with which it is now closely blended.[56]

English aristocracy therefore showed itself flexible and sensitive to changing social and economic conditions. It also realised that, far from recognising it as a progressive move, it had to resist any liberalisation of 'entry qualifications' into the establishment. Throughout the nineteenth century it remained exclusive and demanding. Notwithstanding the necessary marriage of birth with new wealth, it did not allow industrialists easy access to the aristocracy. The first industrial peer was, in fact, the third generation of one of the most illustrious and successful industrial families (the Strutts). Thus the landed nobility continued to maintain the rigid social structure and quasi-ascribed status system of the past whilst at the same time refilling its coffers with 'new' money from the industrial sector.

Conspicuous consumption of the ruling elite grew steadily from 1850 to 1914. In the earlier Victorian years ostentatious display was kept within 'respectable' bounds although spending was at significant levels.[57]

Later in the century, however, and more particularly in the Edwardian era, conspicuous economic expenditure had reached extraordinarily high levels, fuelled by the 'fin de siecle' excesses and example of the Prince of Wales and his entourage, by the emergence of a plutocracy which attempted to buy social recognition in the same way as the nouveaux riches in the United States and by the marked decline in Protestant religious constraint which had been a characteristic of the middle years of Victorian England.

The period 1890–1914 can be considered an era of pronounced conspicuous consumption undertaken by an aristocracy which had survived a hundred years of massive industrial, social and economic change and by their plutocratic allies in power.[58] This alliance served not only the interests of the often financially embarrassed social elite but also the newly arrived plutocrats. The ostentatious lifestyles of the late Victorian and Edwardian years did not, however, go unnoticed at the time. As in the United States, a growing social and political conscience led many commentators to attack the profligacy and conscious waste of the few. The attack in Britain was shaped by the increasing disenchantment with patterns of conspicuous consumption which were in evidence on the other side of the Atlantic. The excesses of the American 'Gilded Age' had generally met with a bad reception in Britain and were considered to reflect a society which had no moral foundation or social stability. Veblen's argument that the new industrial elite in the United States were remarkable only for their vulgarity found ready support in Britain, where vulgarity was equated with 'lack of breeding' and social inferiority:

> In America, enormous wealth—not only beyond the dreams of avarice but in such aggregations of millions as make it inconceivable even to its possessors—has descended upon a tiny group of persons who have exploited the resources of the continent. The first generation accumulated these great possessions in a fierce hand-to-hand conflict in which strength and cunning triumphed and polish and pleasantness of manner and kindliness counted for nothing at all. To the second generation is given the spending of it. There are no feudal or communal responsibilities of social obligation. . . . Religion has become a plaything. . . there is a competition of luxurious display, which, in its more advanced stages, passes into an actual insanity. . . It is a society organised from top to bottom on a 'money' basis with everything else as a side-show.[59]

The attack in Britain focused not on the traditional upper classes—who continued to be conspicuous but who tended to be excused on the grounds of breeding and social worthiness—but on the plutocrats, the newly rich industrialists and entrepreneurs who could show no pedigree or social respectability and who were seen as potential destroyers of moral obligation and social order. This attack was effective enough to ensure that the plutocracy constantly sought alliances with socially acceptable individuals and families and reinforced the wish of the middle classes to gain social rather than financial recognition. Unlike the United States, Britain therefore never experienced a status 'war' between the traditional social elite and the wealthy parvenus who wished to secure social position through financial strength and economic display. Conspicuous behaviour was channelled and controlled to a great extent by the imperatives of social tradition and acceptable behaviour; the excesses of Newport and New York were never repeated in London, where conspicuous display was required to be socially respectable if it was to be effective as a means to status improvement.

Throughout the 1850–1914 period the attitudes and behaviour of the middle class were ambivalent. There was without question a desire to display newly acquired wealth but it did not find any significant expression in conspicuous display. What conspicuous consumption did take place reflected an attempt to copy the lifestyle of the country 'gentlemen' through pretentious building and ornate decoration. There seemed little independent ostentation which was directed at forging a new elite based on industrial prosperity.

The reasons for this overall lack of conspicuous behaviour are several. Firstly, the middle classes never really wanted or felt able to challenge the social superiority of the landed gentry—indeed, they flattered by imitation in the hope of having status conferred on them by the establishment. Secondly, the self-help doctrine, as in the United States, had been a considerable impetus to the entrepreneurial initiatives of the nineteenth century but in Britain the doctrine had never really broken away from the behavioural constraints which the Protestant faith had placed on the display of wealth. Finally, Victorian middle class ambitions had always been directed at establishing one's credentials as a 'gentleman'; this in effect produced a heavy middle class emphasis on education and on securing careers for their children in the professions rather than in trade. Consequently, overt ostentatious display was not seen as a particularly productive pursuit and could be singularly unsuccessful in securing status gains.

The First World War effectively saw the end of the conspicuous excesses which had persisted through the late Victorian and Edwardian eras. As in the United States, the war was a catalyst for even greater social and political change and was also soon followed by a depression which lasted through the 1920s and 1930s and which destroyed many private fortunes together with the economic aspirations of the middle classes. Ostentatious economic display could now become a positive disadvantage as the community's level of tolerance of such behaviour was sharply reduced by the widespread deprivation and poverty of the period.

By 1940 the momentum of the achieving society which had existed since 1700 had largely disappeared. The depression brought a realisation that hard work alone was not a necessary and sufficient condition for individual and community prosperity and a far greater attention was being given to the costs associated with the implementation of an unregulated self-help philosophy. Socialism had arrived as a political force and the gross inequalities of lifestyle and income distribution were coming in for far more searching scrutiny and criticism. Those individuals who did possess the finances to support a life centred on conspicuous expenditure were actively discouraged from so doing by the radically changed social environment and by the economic and political consequences which such behaviour was likely to produce. By the beginning of the Second World War conspicuous consumption on the scale that had been observed in Britain and the United States during the years of self-help, rapid industrialisation and high economic growth was at an end.

There can be no doubt that, as achieving societies, both the United States and Britain experienced levels of conspicuous consumption which were high enough to suggest that ostentatious economic display may be an unavoidable product of achievement oriented societies. Despite inevitable differences in the actual time periods at which conspicuous consumption was most in evidence, there is a similar pattern of events in the experience of both countries when display consumption is plotted against those achievement indicators which gave the impetus to economic growth and development.

The growth of achievement motivation in the United States only became significant after 1830 and grew massively over the 1850–1890 period. In contrast, Britain experienced its greatest rate of growth in achievement stimuli from 1700–1800. Achievement imagery fell sharply in America after 1890 and continued to fall until 1950, whilst in Britain a sharp decline occurred over the 1800–1840 period, followed by a recovery in the Victorian self-help era and then by a renewed decline after 1870.[60] In both countries, however, the level of conspicuous consumption was at its highest in the years immediately after the peaks of achievement indicators. Conspicuous economic excesses were building up in the United States through the 1870s and 1880s but peaked in the twenty years after 1890—the year which saw a dramatic turnaround in achievement motivators and the start of a swift decline in self-help culture and philosophy. In Britain also, conspicuous consumption occurred in two waves which followed the American pattern. The first consumption peak (1800–1830) followed the decline in achievement scores which began in 1800 after one hundred years of high growth rate in such indicators. Secondly, the 'fin de siecle' excesses of the late Victorian and then the Edwardian periods followed the achievement indicator decline which set in after 1870 following the 1840–1870 self-help revival.

It would appear, therefore, that conspicuous consumption in the two societies was at its greatest not during but immediately after sustained periods of high achievement motivation—i.e. there would seem to be a strong correlation between achievement indicators and conspicuous economic behaviour if a time lag of up to thirty years is allowed.

Although a strong, lagged correlation is detectable for both Britain and the United States, the relationship is complicated by the fact that the motivation for ostentatious economic behaviour in the two societies would appear to have been markedly different. In the United States conspicuous consumption was clearly undertaken in the 1870–1910 period by newly rich industrialists and their heirs who lacked any ascribed status and who were seeking to achieve status for the first time by the ostentatious display of wealth. Their conspicuous excesses were an attempt to overthrow the traditional ascribed-status system and to supplant it with one based on money and wealth. In contrast, British conspicuous consumption of the 1800–1830 period was undertaken not by industrialists and merchants hoping to end ascribed power and privilege but by the 'traditional' landowning elite who were seeking to reinforce the existing ascriptive social system. The 1890–1910 period was dominated by the same ascribed-status elite—whose land based wealth, however, had been seriously declining in the early and mid-Victorian years—in alliance with the new industrial plutocrats who, unlike their American counterparts, were in no real sense at war with the existing ascriptive system of social ranking but rather were seeking to establish newly acquired wealth as an acceptable alternative path to social status and prestige.

Due in no small part to the contrasting social and economic histories of the two countries, the stimulus to spending was very different—one the wish to attack and destroy, the other to reinforce or to seek accommodation within existing orders of social status. The more radical intention of American conspicuous consumers is reflected in the far more outrageous levels of ostentatious display and waste which were observed over the 1890–1910 period—levels so high that they drew worldwide comment and criticism.

Conspicuous consumption thrived in the United States for many reasons. Firstly, the ascribed-status elite were less secure than their counterparts in Britain. Their position of privilege derived from the colonial tradition which had no real roots in the United States—and they were thus vulnerable to attack from homegrown, self-made men of achievement. Secondly, the levels of discretionary income and wealth enjoyed by the American industrial barons were so enormous that the financial ammunition for an all-out attack was always available in abundance—an advantage never enjoyed to anything like the same degree by the British plutocracy. . . Finally, there was a latent religious and cultural approval of wealth-making both in Britain and the United States throughout the nineteenth century but the latter actively encouraged the subsequent display of wealth and material possessions and awarded social recognition in large measure on this apparent evidence of a productive and constructive life. The British attitude to ostentatious display was never as positive or rewarding.

In both societies, hard evidence of the reaction of the emergent middle classes and other social groups to conspicuous consumption at the top of the social and economic register is in short supply. Certainly, the distribution of income and wealth remained sufficiently unequal to ensure that conspicuous expenditure on any significant scale (and measured in absolute money terms) was the preserve of the rich few, but it is reasonable to conclude from historical observation that, notwithstanding the rapid social and economic changes of the nineteenth century, the level of resentment shown to such spending by the less fortunate was never intolerably high. This was particularly so in the United States where conspicuous excesses were faithfully reported by the press and received with interest and implicit approval by its readers. Only after 1900—when conspicuous economic behaviour had reached proportions generally held to be unjustified by any criterion and when Veblen and others were openly attacking the extravagance and waste of the period— did public opinion turn significantly against conspicuous consumption. But there is little doubt that throughout the Gilded Age, the 'pecuniary emulation' cited by Veblen was a reality and evident at most if not all levels of American society. The display of wealth was firmly established as an acceptable means of social advancement by all social groups.

In Britain, the reaction was more complicated. Excessive conspicuous display on the part of ascribed-status consumers was tolerated far more than that undertaken by achieved-status seekers—a reaction which underlines the fact that British industrial expansion took place, by consent, within a predominantly ascriptive system. Vertical social advancement through wealth display was never accepted on the American scale and the conspicuous consumption undertaken by the British middle classes was always relatively restrained. However, whilst refusing to concede vertical (i.e. between class) status advances on the basis of ostentatious economic display, what evidence we have suggests that horizontal (i.e. within class) status competition based on conspicuous consumption was quite marked in the various middle class groupings and there was considerable status striving within clearly defined and recognised social boundaries.

Overall, whilst 'emulation' seems to have been observed in both countries and in most social groups, the vertical incentive to progress socially seems to have been more culturally acceptable and therefore more in evidence in the United States. Given the less tradition bound society which existed at that time in America, this observation is not surprising. However, it is possible to overstate the degree of vertically directed consumption which occurred in the Gilded Age. The earlier period (1870–1890) was primarily motivated by attacks on the traditional 'aristocracy' by the new industrial elites and ostentatious spending could be considered to have vertical social objectives. After 1890, however, much conspicuous consumption was 'horizontal' as the new rich competed with each other and, in attempting to secure within-group ascendancy, introduced a ratchet effect on conspicuous economic waste which reached alarming proportions after 1900. If the lower social groups emulated not only the economic behaviour of the elites but also their motivations, then the shift from vertical to horizontal competition probably extended throughout the social spectrum and approximated more closely to the British pattern of ostentatious display.

The considerable differences between the American and British experiences over the 1700–1940 period make it difficult to generalise about the nature and incidence of conspicuous consumption in achieving societies. However, some tentative conclusions may be drawn.

Firstly, the 'lagged' relationship between high economic achievement motivations and conspicuous expenditure levels suggests that maximum ostentatious display occurs primarily after wealth has been accumulated and not during the actual process of wealth-making. This of course is a sensible economic decision on the part of the conspicuous consumer but such behaviour does suggest that gains in social status through economic display are second order rather than first order incentives to wealth production and are not primary incentives to financial prosperity. It would therefore appear that conspicuous consumption becomes attractive as a strategy when the potential consumer has already achieved a significant economic advantage over his social competitors and wishes to translate such advantage into a status gain.

Secondly, the evidence suggests that observed conspicuous consumption produces 'pecuniary emulation' in others and generates cultural and social acceptance of this means to status improvement or consolidation. However, there would also appear to be a socially imposed limit to ostentatious display after which conspicuous economic behaviour becomes counterproductive and status changes become negative rather than positive. There may well be a consumption cycle in such societies, therefore, in which conspicuous display is initiated by an economically advantaged group; is emulated by others (who must feel that the 'open' society makes it possible for them to use income and wealth gains as a way to improve their own social position), builds up to socially divisive levels as vertically motivated consumption is reinforced by far greater levels of horizontal competition; and finally subsides as social protest increases.

If this interpretation is correct, it would suggest that wealth relativities rather than income relativities are the prime motivators of conspicuous consumption and this conclusion in turn has some important consequences. Status gains based on accumulated wealth are significantly different from those based on income in that the former are awarded on a potentially ascriptive basis—that is, they may be passed on from generation to generation—whilst the latter are made on the evidence of economic superiority at one particular point in time and therefore are entirely achievement-centred with no possibility of long term ascriptive status unless and until the high income can be converted into substantial accumulated wealth. Following this argument, it would appear that the explanation for ostentatious economic display not being significantly in evidence during the process of wealth accumulation (witness the American and British experience) lies in the fact that conspicuous consumers may in reality be seeking long term ascribed-status rather than short term achieved-status gains.

It has been argued for many years that achieved-status distinctions should be more frequent in rapidly growing economies and ascribed-status distinctions more common in slowly developing (i.e. traditional) societies. A low stress on ascribed status has often been considered a necessary cause or accompaniment of economic development. Theoretically, therefore, potential achieved-status gains should be the principal motivator—particularly of conspicuous consumers—in any achieving society and socially directed consumption should not be shaped to any significant degree by ascribed-status considerations.

The evidence would appear to contradict this theoretical proposition in so far as conspicuous consumption is concerned. British ostentatious display of the nineteenth century was dominated by ascribed-status holders seeking, presumably, to reinforce their ascriptive social superiority (based on title and 'old money'). And in the United States, a country lacking any historically entrenched traditional elite or formal social class structure, the 'generation gap' between income creation (low conspicuous consumption) and accumulated wealth (high conspicuous consumption) suggests that future ascribed-status considerations may have been underlying (possibly subconsciously) the ostentatious display of the period. (A cursory glance at the present day social register in the United States would, in fact, reassure most status motivated conspicuous consumers of the Gilded Age that their long term strategy—if such it was—was a success.) Whilst the social position of the colonial elite was never destroyed, the descendants of nineteenth century new money today have status clearly ascribed to them on the basis of family name and inheritance and now themselves seem immune from the attacks of any future conspicuous consumers.

Empirical research directed at exploring—inter alia—the relative importance of achieved and ascribed-status distinctions in achieving societies has found no significant relationship between achieved status and economic development. Social achievement neither precedes nor accompanies periods of rapid economic advance and high achievement motivation.[61] It seems reasonable, therefore, to entertain the proposition that sustained conspicuous consumption by those who have accumulated wealth may be seen as an investment to secure long term ascribed-status gains rather than as an expenditure intended solely to maximise current achieved-status recognition. If this is so, the distinction between conspicuous consumption in traditional societies and in achieving societies becomes less significant in so far as the motivation for such behaviour is concerned.

Notes

1 McClelland, D.C., *The Achieving Society*, Van Nostrand, Princeton, 1961.

2 As examples, see Hofstadter, R., *The Millionaire Industrialists*, in Hofstadter, R., 'The American Political Tradition', A. Knopf, New York, pp.162-7; Morris, L., *The 400*, in Morris, L., 'Postscript to Yesterday', Random House, New York, 1947, pp.7-13; Saarinen, A.B., *The Proud Possessors*, Random House, New York, 1958, pp.58-62; Lord, W., *The Good Years: From 1900 to the First World War*, Longmans, London, 1960.

3 McGiffert, M. and Skotheim, R.A., *American Social Thought: Sources and Interpretations*, vol.1, Addison-Wesley, California, 1972, p.8.

4 Lipset, S.M., *The First New Nation*, Heinemann, London, 1963, especially Chapter 3, 'A Changing American Character'.

5 The Gilded Age was at its height in the period 1870—1900 although broader definitions (1860—1910) are found in social and economic history literature. Certainly the period 1900—1910 was conspicuous in terms of excessive consumption but after 1900 the gilt was clearly beginning to tarnish.

6 McClelland, D.C., op.cit., p.150.

7 Furnas, J.C., *The Americans—A Social History of the United States 1587—1914*, Longman, London, 1969, p.606.

8 Hofstadter, R., *The Age of Reform*, Jonathan Cape, London, 1962, p.136.

9 Hofstadter, R., op.cit., p.136.

10 The need to achieve a fast rate of economic development itself reflected a cultural bias which was to encourage conspicuous consumption at a much later date.

11   Thoreau, H.D., *Walden,* Boston, 1854.

12   'Self-help' attempted to reflect the ethical assumptions of a new type of society. Its message was clear and simple: 'The spirit of self-help is the root of all genuine growth in the individual; and exhibited in the lives of man, it constitutes the true source of national vigour and strength. Help from without is often enfeebling in its effects but help from within invariably invigorates. Whatever is done for men or classes, to a certain extent takes away the stimulus and necessity of doing for themselves; and where men are subject to over-guidance and over-government, the inevitable tendency is to render them comparatively helpless'. (Samuel Smiles, *Self-Help,* London, 1859, Chapter X).

See also, Harrison, J.F.C., 'The Victorian Gospel of Success', *Victorian Studies,* I, 1957, pp.155-64 and Briggs, A., *Victorian People,* Chicago, 1955.

13   See, for instance, Garfield, D.J., *Elements of Success,* in Hindale, B.A. (ed), 'President Garfield and Education', Boston, 1882. Also Alger, H. (Jn), *John Oakley's Inheritance,* Boston, 1869.

14   Quoted in Furnas, J.C., op.cit., p.648.

15   Hofstadter, R., op.cit., p.138.

16   See Miller, W., 'American Historians and the Business Elite' in *Journal of Economic History,* vol.IX, November 1949, pp.184-208; Miller, W., 'The Recruitment of the American Business Elite', *Quarterly Journal of Economics,* vol.LXIV, May 1950, pp.242-53; C. Wright Mills, 'The American Business Elite: A Collective Portrait', *Journal of Economic History,* vol.V, 1945, pp.20-44.

17   Weiss, R., *The American Myth of Success: From Horatio Alger to Norman Vincent Peale,* Basic Books, New York, 1969; Wohl, R.R., *The Country Boy Myth and its Place in American Urban Culture,* in Rischin, M. (ed), 'Perspectives in American History', Charles Warren Centre for Studies in American History, III, Harvard, 1969, pp.77-156; Hofstadter, R., *The Millionaire Industrialists,* op.cit., pp.162-7.

18   Ratner, S., *American Taxation,* New York, 1942, pp.136, 275.

19   Shearman, T.G. *The Coming Billionaire,* 1891.

20   Morris, L., *The 400,* op.cit., pp.7-13.

21   Hofstadter, R., *The Age of Reform,* op.cit., p.138.

22   Furnas, J.C., op.cit., p.604.

23   Howe, E.W., *The Story of a Country Town,* 1883; Kirkland, J., *Zury,* 1887; Garland, H., *Main-Travelled Road,* 1891.

24 Howell, *A Hazard of New Fortunes,* 1890; Riis, J., *How the Other Half Lives,* 1890.

25 Carnegie, A., 'Wealth', *North American Review,* CXLVIII, June, 1889, pp.653-64.

26 The dramatic build up in ostentatious display which occurred after 1890 was clearly the stimulus to Veblen's *Theory of the Leisure Class* published in 1899.

27 Miller, W., *The Realm of Wealth,* in Higham, J. (ed) 'The Reconstruction of American History', Hutchinson, London, 1962, p.141.

28 See, for example, Phillips, D.G., *The Reign of Gilt,* New York, 1905, pp.190-6; Reeve, A.B., 'The Prevention of Poverty', *World's Week,* 15, 1908; Moxom, P.S., 'The Child and Social Reform', *North American Review,* 192, December 1910; Poole, E., *Disease is Preventable and Curable,* 1903.

29 Sage, R., *Ambition to Rise in Life: Never by Luck,* in Marden, O.S., 'Talks with Great Workers', New York, 1901, pp.18-22.

30 Weyl, W.E., *The New Democracy, An Essay on Certain Political and Economic Tendencies in the United States,* New York, 1912.

31 Schlesinger, A.M., *The Rise of Modern America 1865—1951,* Macmillan, New York, 1951, p.240.

32 See, for example, Smuts, R.W., *European Impressions of the American Workers,* King's Crown Press, New York, 1953, p.13.

33 McCready, B., 'On the Influence of Trades, Professions and Occupations in the United States in the Production of Disease', Transactions of the Medical Society of the State of New York (1836—1837), III, pp.146-7.

34 Lipset, S.M., op.cit., p.112.

35 Brogan, D.W., *The English People,* Hamish Hamilton, London, 1943, p.99.

36 Brogan, D.W., *USA: An Outline of the Country, its People and Institutions,* Oxford University Press, New York, 1941, pp.116-7.

37 In choosing Britain as a comparative study, the considerable social and cultural differences are acknowledged. However, it is clearly impossible to find two entirely identical social systems for purposes of comparison. The US—British comparison is legitimate in the sense that both countries share a common language and that, to some considerable extent, nineteenth century American culture was a derivative—albeit radical and rejectionist—of the older British tradition.

38 McClelland, D., op.cit., p.133.

39 Ramsey, P., *Tudor Economic Problems*, Gollancz, London, 1963, pp.122 and 140.

40 Mingay, G.E., *English Landed Society in the Eighteenth Century*, Routledge and Kegan Paul, Toronto, 1963.

41 Ibid., p.211.

42 Bryant, A., *The Age of Elegance*, Collins, London, 1950, p.311.

43 Gore, J., (ed), *Creevey—Life and Times*, 1934.

44 Bryant, A., op.cit., p.315.

45 Ibid., p.313.

46 Simond, L., *Journal of a Tour of Residence in Great Britain During the Years 1810 and 1811*, 1815.

47 McClelland, D., op.cit.

48 Ibid., p.148.

49 Ibid., p.142.

50 Ibid., p.139, especially figure 4.3.

51 Throughout the early period of the Industrial Revolution—and through perhaps to the self-help period after 1860—the newly emergent middle classes, enjoying wealth derived from the process of industrialisation, give perhaps the best example of uncomplicated 'pecuniary emulation'. Their behaviour was markedly ingratiating, a factor which reassured the aristocratic elite in their conspicuous lifestyles.

52 Black, E.C. (ed), *Victorian Culture and Society*, Harper and Row, New York, 1973, p.155.

53 Burn, W.L., quoted in Best, G., *Victorian Britain 1851—1875*, Weidenfield and Nicholson, London, 1971.

54 Best, G., op.cit.

55 Seaman, L.C.B., *Victorian England*, Methuen, London, 1973, p.263.

56 Escott, T.H.S., *England: Her People, Polity and Pursuits*, New York, 1880, pp.317-25.

57 The reticence of conspicuous consumers between 1830 and 1850 is largely explained by the radical political changes and uncertainties of the period. Financial discretion overcame the desire for ostentatious display, particularly after the 1832 Reform Bill seemed to herald dramatic shifts in the balance of political and economic power:

> The Reform Bill of 1832. . . . has substituted, in a very large degree, the prestige of achievement for the prestige of

position. The mere men of fashion, the fops, dandies and exquisites, the glories of whose life was indolence, and who looked upon any thing in the way of occupation as a disgrace, have gone out of date never to return. Before 1832, there existed a society in England very like the old exclusive society of Vienna. The chief and indeed almost only road to it lay through politics, and politics were for the most part a rigidly aristocratic profession. . . . The Reform Bill admitted an entirely new element into political life, and threw open the whole of the political arena (reference Escott, op.cit.).

In fact, the radical intentions of the Reform Bill were never, de facto, achieved in the Victorian years and by 1850 the traditional social and political elite—still very much in power—felt confident enough to raise their levels of conspicuous consumption.

58 Camplin, J., *The Rise of the Plutocrats,* Constable, London, 1978.

59 Masterman, C.F.G., *The Condition of England,* Shenval Press, London, 1909, Chapter 2, 'The Conquerors'.

60 McClelland, D., op.cit., pp.139 and 150.

61 McClelland, D., op.cit., p.184.

6 Conspicuous consumption in affluent societies

The achievement oriented societies created in America and Britain during their rapid economic development had produced mature industrial states by the middle of the twentieth century. However, the social and economic changes which were first in evidence in the United States after 1945 led many observers to believe that the affluence created in reaching industrial maturity, together with the inevitable technological advances made during the process of development, created conditions under which a new type of society—the 'affluent society'—was beginning to emerge.[1]

The abundance of wealth and the relatively high levels of prosperity are seen to be only a part of the effects of the industrialisation process. Society becomes heavily urbanised, traditional social barriers are removed as job mobility increases and social relationships tend to become more impersonal. High levels of capital investment and technological skills are built up during the period of transitional growth. A new middle class emerges—typified by the salaried employee in business. Eventually there is a noticeable decline in the numbers and in the proportion of the population who work in production and extraction and an increase in those employed in white-collar work and the service trades.[2]

As affluence builds up, people tend to become more literate and there is a substantial increase in educational opportunities and in attained education standards. Increased wealth and the redistribution of income tend to ensure provision of the basic essentials of life and people are likely to turn increasingly to the tertiary economic sector to purchase service goods. As a result, the service industries prosper. There is overall a greater opportunity for leisure and a greater financial ability to enjoy it.

Perhaps the greatest single change which is experienced in highly developed, technologically advanced countries is the proliferation of new communication channels within the community as a whole and the importance which communication—often from impersonal and previously unknown sources—comes to play in the individual's life and lifestyle. There is a far greater consumption of words and images from the mass media once a society reaches an advanced industrialised state. Hence, the distribution of words from urban centres which is a feature of developing, achieving communities is rapidly expanded and comes to play a far more significant role in affluent, fully industrialised societies. Communication networks multiply dramatically, new media forms are introduced, and the individual is increasingly exposed to the opinions, values and thoughts of others in his community.

The cumulative effect of these social, economic and technological changes has been the subject of considerable research and discussion over the past twenty years. Although the United States was the first society to experience such changes and to try to adjust to them, similar developments have occurred—and are occurring—in many other highly industrialised states throughout the world. Again, recent American and European experience in particular can be taken as indicative of the social and economic transition to be expected in any society undergoing the changeover from achievement motivated economic development to post industrial affluence.

It would be an impossible task to try to identify and evaluate all consequences of the transition process outlined above. However, for the purposes of this study, it is necessary only to examine those factors which can reasonably be expected to have a significant influence on the relative attractiveness of conspicuous consumption and also on the size and direction such consumption patterns might take. Of primary importance in this respect is the impact of social and economic change on the relationship of the individual with the other members of his community, particularly in so far as it will cause him to reassess his consumption behaviour.

There is today general agreement that the increased urbanisation of the workforce, the greater job mobility and the greatly increased levels of communication between organisations and people who hitherto had no direct or indirect contact, have all combined to ensure that the individual in the affluent society is far more 'socialised' than his counterparts in traditional or developing communities:

> The individual learns to respond to signals from a far wider circle than is constituted by his parents. The family is no longer a closely knit unit to which he belongs but merely part of a wider social environment to which he becomes attentive. In these respects, he resembles the tradition-directed persons:

both live in a group milieu and lack the inner-directed person's capacity to go it alone. The nature of this group milieu, however, differs radically in the two cases. The other-directed person is cosmopolitan. For him the border between the familiar and the strange—a border clearly marked in the societies depending on tradition-direction—has broken down. As the family continuously absorbs the strange and so re-shapes itself, so the strange becomes familiar. While the inner-directed person could be 'at home abroad' by virtue of his relative insensitivity to others, the other-directed person is, in a sense, at home everywhere and nowhere, capable of a superficial intimacy with and response to every-one.[3]

These generalisations on social priorities and responses in an affluent society would seem acceptable. There is little doubt that peer groups have indeed come to be a major source of reference for the individual in the modern world, although the shift away from inner-directed to other-directed values is not as swift or dramatic as was once supposed. There is evidence to suggest that throughout the 1950s—accepted as the first affluent society decade in the United States—a significant proportion of the newly prosperous middle and working classes in fact retained an achievement philosophy based on self-help and personal enterprise. Only after 1960 did a more socially oriented value system come to form a significant part of the social character.

The socialisation of individual attitudes and beliefs can be assumed to have a considerable influence on actual and potential conspicuous consumers. The emphasis on peer group relationships suggests that vertical status drives become less attractive and that within-group status objectives are reinforced. However, the need to belong or 'relate' to a peer group may well require conformity rather than individual ostentation and this could serve to ensure that conspicuous consumption would serve no useful purpose in securing prestige within a particular reference group. If there is a genuine move from vertical to horizontal motivation and the peer group or groups to which the individual responds insist on a conformity of behaviour, then 'pure' conspicuous consumption should theoretically decline in importance.

In the early 1950s many observers had little doubt that the motivation for high levels of conspicuous consumption in the newly affluent societies would ultimately be lost. Veblen's conspicuous consumer was seen to be playing a role demanded of him by his position, or by the position to which he aspired, in an achieved-status society and was therefore engaged in an externalised rivalry with other individuals who were competing for similar status gains. The affluent society consumer might compete in what seems to be very much the same way, it was argued, but only to the degree that the reference groups to which he responds require him to do so:

> His desire to outshine, as we should expect from his mode of peer-group socialisation, is very much muted and is allowed expression only to the degree that popularity depends on success in marginal innovation and in differentiation in consumption.[4]

Expectations of a decline in the relative attractiveness of conspicuous consumption as a means to status improvement could be further supported by the observed rise in importance, in status terms, of a new factor which had come to play a significant role in determining social prestige—that of education. Post-war affluence saw the emergence of a new 'Diploma Elite' and social position came to be determined more and more by the possession of a college diploma of some sort.[5] A majority of commentators saw a clear hardening of social divisions based on different levels of educational attainment. This new development could firstly be expected to convince people of the importance of ensuring that their children grew to appreciate the social need for a good education and secondly that their own attempts to 'buy' status gains through conspicuous economic display were becoming increasingly unproductive.

Whilst these several social factors work against the interests of conspicuous consumption, many other developments in the post-industrial society seem to create an environment which could encourage such behaviour. Firstly, there is a marked change in public attitudes towards social and economic equality. The conspicuous consumers of the late nineteenth century, both in the United States and, to a lesser extent, in Britain, had finally been persuaded that their conspicuous excesses were becoming ineffective because the inequalities of wealth and income were causing a groundswell of public resentment against their activities. The changing social and political climate of the period was producing demands that the rich and privileged should redistribute or share their wealth with those less fortunate. The nineteenth century notion that poverty was a punishment for incompetence or sloth was increasingly rejected after 1900 and the case for a substantial redistribution of income and wealth gained in importance. However, the preoccupation with egalitarianism which effectively damped down conspicuous consumption in the inter-war years did not survive the Second World War. As Galbraith commented in 1977:

> Few things are more evident in modern social history than the decline of interest in inequality as an economic issue. Progressive income tax, long recognised as the most effective available mechanism for redistributing income, was used less and less in such a role after 1950 but this did not produce any

substantial adverse reaction from the general public.[6]

Several explanations for this apparent reduction in concern for further reducing the degree of inequality—still significant in the post-war years— have been put forward. Firstly, most political decisions to reduce inequality taken after periods of rapid economic development stem from the fear that the great inequalities which arise in the process of industrialisation could produce social diversions so great that the stability of society could be threatened by violence. This, of course, is the classic Marxist prediction and depends for its validity on the existence of a considerable resentment of individual wealth, but the evidence of recent years suggests that, if envy does build up, it only operates efficiently as regards near neighbours (in economic terms) and is rarely directed at those of far higher social and economic status.[7] Consequently, the political need to launch an economic attack on the very rich is much reduced.

Secondly, preoccupation with inequality is lessened because it becomes increasingly obvious that the power and privileges of the wealthy are significantly reduced by the very nature of the society which emerges from the industrialisation process. Political privileges are removed from individuals and families who in earlier years had used their wealth to secure favours and preferential treatment from the government of the time. Although wealth still retains an importance in seeking to secure public office—and this is particularly true of the United States—the legislative function of government gains an independence from the self-interest of the rich. Once this independence is seen to exist a part of the case for greater equality of income and wealth is removed.

A third reason for the reduction in concern about inequality is associated with corporate rather than political change. The achieving society, with its emphasis on reward for individual effort, tends to concentrate commercial and industrial power in the hands of a few rich men—a power which in effect gives the wealthy industrial and commercial elites control over the people who work for them in the capitalist system of enterprise. The affluent society, however, sees the arrival of a new, less personal system of business organisation which dramatically reduces the ability of any one individual to alone determine either company policy or the rights and privileges of others.[8]

The removal of absolute corporate power from the very rich means in effect that they also become far less visible as individuals. There seems little doubt that resentment of business leaders is to some extent a function of their frequency of exposure to the general public as men wielding considerable economic power over others; as this visibility reduces, therefore, so again does a part of the hostility to the unequal division of wealth and incomes.

Finally, in all affluent communities there is an inevitable long term

105

redistribution of wealth which offers far greater levels of security and financial independence to the middle and working classes. This greater security in turn damps down the high levels of resentment which can build up against income and wealth inequalities when a majority of individuals feel both deprived and insecure. The arrival of the 'welfare state'—a characteristic of most affluent societies—can therefore work to reduce hostility both towards the retained wealth of the very rich and towards the inequalities of incomes within particular socio-economic classes.

Experience of affluent societies to date has therefore shown that whilst certain changes in social stratification and in social character formation may cause individuals to reassess their behaviour with respect to status achievement and consolidation and would appear to diminish the role of conspicuous consumption as a means to securing status gains, the overall economic and social environment tends to become less rather than more hostile to overt display of income and wealth inequalities. This latter development can, of course, be seen as a natural consequence of the former—i.e. the reduced importance of conspicuous consumption in status terms could lead to a predictable lessening in resentment of such behaviour and a greater tolerance of the conspicuous consumer who is now assumed to be merely wasting his money and securing no social advantage by his ostentatious economic display.

If this interpretation is correct, it can be argued that, notwithstanding the creation of a 'sympathetic' social and economic environment, the motivation to conspicuously consume in affluent societies is considerably reduced. This view has in fact been put forward and supported, more especially in so far as the behaviour of the very rich is concerned. In the United States and Britain, for example, the industrial depressions of the 1920s and 1930s seem to have persuaded the rich that it was ill advised to indulge in ostentatious consumption and they adopted a greater discretion in personal expenditure over this period. In the affluent years following the end of the Second World War, however, whilst the opportunity to conspicuously consume has remained significantly high for the rich and the potential resentment of such behaviour has probably lessened, the 'Gilded Age' excesses of earlier years have not reappeared and the wealthy elites may well have looked for alternative paths to ensure and protect their status in society.

The principal reason put forward to explain the decline in the conspicuous display of wealth by the very rich is that such display loses its effectiveness as the opportunity to behave ostentatiously is enjoyed by far greater numbers of people, thus reducing its importance as an indicator of achieved social position. As the rich become more numerous, their scarcity value inevitably decreases in accordance with the natural laws of supply and demand. Furthermore, the wider opportunity for conspicuous display may tend to make the rich feel that the purchase of expensive goods as a status gesture is becoming increasingly common-place and that alternative channels of status consolidation would be more productive. Galbraith identified this rejectionist trend in the United States:

> Once a significantly impressive display of diamonds could create attention for they signified membership of a highly privileged caste. Now the same diamonds are afforded by a television star or talented harlot. Modern mass communications, especially the movies and television, ensure that the populace at large will see the most lavish caparisoning on the bodies not only of the daughters of the rich but also on the daughters of coal miners and commercial travellers who have struck it rich by their own talents or some facsimile thereof.[9]

Far from indulging in conspicuous display which increasingly fails to distinguish them from others who enjoy similar levels of wealth and income, the upper classes—in total contrast—may react by adopting a posture of 'conspicuous reserve' and develop consumption patterns which are remarkable more for their deliberate lack of ostentation than for their economic profligacy and flamboyance. In so doing, they are implicitly recognising that conspicuous consumption is no longer effec-tive as a means of status reinforcement and are attempting to ensure that resort to conspicuous economic display is self-defeating for the rich 'newcomers' of the modern affluent societies.[10]

Although the very rich may well find less reward in status-directed ostentatious display and so cut back on their efforts in this direction, in post-industrial communities they are no longer the only group of poten-tial and significant conspicuous consumers. The substantial new purchas-ing power enjoyed for the first time by middle class and working class people makes conspicuous consumption available to status-minded individuals at all social levels. Whilst the highest socio-economic groups may reduce their economic display behaviour, therefore, we need to consider how attractive such behaviour becomes to other social groups and how they react to the opportunities presented to them. . . .

Notwithstanding the reduced emphasis on 'traditional' class values and the increased importance of peer and reference groups, social class barriers may well crystallise in the affluent societies. The process of industrialisation and wealth creation which characterises achievement-motivated nations appears to harden rather than soften social strata. Britain and continental Europe had a strong class system well before industrialisation and the development process has seen neither the demise of ascribed status nor the removal of non-financial barriers to social mobility. Given the starting point of such achieving societies and the historically entrenched 'caste systems' which had operated for several hundred years, this result is not entirely surprising. However, a similar degree of social rigidity has also developed in the United States—a country with a weak tradition of social class divisions and stratification. Social mobility has, in the view of many, been significantly reduced by the clearly defined class distinctions which are now primarily on the basis of two particularly dominant socio-economic factors—those of occupation and education.

The affluent society rules under which much status would appear to be awarded on the basis of factors other than income or accumulated wealth would seem to ensure that for all social groups conspicuous consumption would be ineffective in securing a significant social prestige and position within a particular community. However, this is not the case. The emphasis on occupation and education certainly brings about changes in the reward system and in the distribution of income and wealth away from the self-made entrepreneur and towards the new diploma and administrative elites but with respect to status conference a problem similar to that facing the newly rich industrialists of the achieving societies is in turn posed for this new 'aristocracy'. For although social status would, in an ideal affluent society, be awarded purely on evidence of merit gained through the nature of an individual's employment and through his standard of literacy and schooling, the reality is such that the rewards given to educational and occupational success have to be 'revealed' in order for the status to be conferred. In such circumstances, conspicuous consumption is available as a means of bridging the gap between status qualification and subsequent status recognition.

Ostentatious economic display, therefore, can survive the arrival of meritocracy and may remain relevant and effective in societies which are committed to reducing the importance of wealth as a factor in securing social prestige and position. Whilst the very rich and the old upper classes may feel such behaviour to be passé, the middle class in particular, anxious to press its status claims on the basis of non-entrepreneurial achievement within a post-industrial society, often needs to resort to such display as a means to social recognition.

Conspicuous consumption is therefore a recognisable element of middle class behaviour in affluent societies. However, the pattern of economic display can be expected to be fundamentally different from the extravagant excesses encouraged in 'earlier' forms of social and economic organisation. Middle class conspicuous expenditure is made attractive as a means of reward display for individuals who are primarily concerned with asserting occupational and educational standing and this primary motivation will itself have a strong influence on the particular pattern of conspicuous display adopted by the consumer. Emphasis on the importance of education in particular should direct purchasers towards revealing not only their financial rewards but also their 'taste' in product choice. The criterion on which status is de facto awarded will be expected to be reflected in the quality of consumer preferences; revealed taste is therefore as important to the consumer—and to his audience—as revealed income or wealth.

The above distinction is important because it introduces a new element into the conspicuous consumption decision. Whilst the 'pure' conspicuous consumer of the traditional and achieving societies was (and is) indiscriminate in that only the act of wealth display has any social significance for him, the status seeking consumer in the affluent society often has to bring a far greater selectivity to bear on his purchase decision. To this extent, price (or cost) can no longer be the sole criterion on which decisions must be based and the consumer needs additional knowledge of the probable audience reaction to his purchase in so far as it reveals his taste and the social quality of his preferences.

The importance of conspicuous economic display to those who have meritocratic claims to status recognition can therefore be established. However, there exists a further significant group of potential consumers who may choose to conspicuously consume for different reasons in order to achieve the same basic social objective of status improvement. The emergence of a meritocratic elite has the effect of isolating those who have not in fact received a high standard of education or who do not enjoy an occupation which confers any significant social prestige. Such individuals are clearly at a social disadvantage but may nevertheless still look for ways of making substantial status gains. Whilst they can not compete 'legitimately' on the basis of educational or occupational attainment, conspicuous consumption offers an effective alternative route to status improvement.

To understand why this should be so, it is necessary to stress again the division between the theory and the reality of status award in affluent societies. It has already been seen that although social status would ideally be awarded on merit gained through the nature of an individual's employment and through his achieved literacy and schooling, the reality is such that the rewards given to educational and occupational success have to be revealed in order for status to be conferred. It is this need to resort to the surrogate of money and wealth which flaws the system as far as the meritocrats are concerned because the opportunity for economic ostentation is given not only to the 'legitimate' elite but also to all those who enjoy a level of wealth, income or credit sufficient for them to conspicuously consume. In other words, whilst conspicuous consumption is a necessary expression of achieved status, it is available to any individual who can command the necessary financial resources and consequently can not discriminate between purchasers on the basis of occupation or education.

Ostentatious economic display can therefore serve to mask socio-economic shortcomings and, in so doing, can help all consumers motivated by vertical status objectives to secure some recognition from higher social groups. The possibility of success is improved by the vastly increased geographic mobility which is evident in affluent consumer societies—a mobility which creates a far more impersonal network of social relationships. It is quite possible, for example, that individuals or families living in close geographic proximity to one another may have little or no knowledge of their respective occupations or educational standing and this social isolation produces ideal conditions for the 'unqualified' status seeker to use conspicuous consumption as a (false) surrogate for a social position he does not in theory merit.

In an attempt to protect the legitimate status seeker, the meritocracy may hope to isolate and identify fraudulent claimants by laying heavy emphasis on one particular aspect of conspicuous consumption which has already been referred to as a necessary element of status-directed ostentatious display in affluent societies—that of revealed taste. 'Good taste' may be assumed to be a characteristic common only to those who come from a 'correct' family or occupational background or who have received an education of sufficient substance to enable them to make selective purchase decisions on the basis of relative social and aesthetic quality. Given this assumption, revealed taste could, in theory at least, be used to confirm those who have justified claims to such prestige. In practice, however, the usefulness of consumer taste as a criterion for social stratification is much reduced; the proposition that taste is uniquely a function of socio-economic background and education cannot be defended in so far as consumer oriented, post-industrial societies are concerned. Mass communication ensures frequent media exposure of the social and economic behaviour of all groups and information on relative consumption patterns is therefore readily available, allowing easy access to the detail of taste and quality judgements made by each social class and reference group.

The above analysis has argued that conspicuous consumption can survive and prosper in affluent societies notwithstanding the introduction of a prestige system based theoretically on achieved occupational and educational status. Potential consumers would appear to fall into two principal groups. Firstly, existing and new members of diploma and administrative elites find it necessary to consolidate their status through socially approved and acceptable conspicuous display. Such consumption is predominantly horizontal (i.e. within-group) in that it seeks no substantial vertical (between-group) advantage involving a move from a lower to a higher status group. The second group comprises those who may have some (limited) occupational and educational prestige (typically those employed in white-collar rather than blue-collar jobs and with a recognisable but insubstantial education which stops short of being acceptable to the diploma elites) and who actively strive to secure vertical rather than horizontal status gains.

This latter group can be more precisely identified; it represents those who are often classified as the 'lower middle class' and whose status-sensitivity is heightened because of their particular position on the social scale. Above them they see the middle class proper who enjoy the status rewards of successful meritocrats—a group they very much aspire to join; below them, the working class, a group from whom they actively seek to distance themselves by any means at their disposal.[11]

Conspicuous consumption in the affluent societies therefore becomes very much a middle class (or pseudo middle class) phenomenon. In looking at the lower working classes, both in the United States and in Europe, there is little evidence to suggest that status considerations play any important or enduring role in their consumption patterns—on the contrary, they seem particularly disinterested in matters of prestige and social standing outside their own milieu. This may result from the very heavy emphasis placed on occupation by the working class—an emphasis which persuades them that conspicuous consumption would in no way be effective in diminishing the gap between themselves and the broadly defined middle class. Again, the cultural barriers between the two groups—barriers linked to occupation and education—may deter the working class generally from seeking to 'join the opposition' for fear of alienating their existing peer groups. For vertically-directed conspicuous consumption to occur, the many emotional and social obligations holding an individual to his place in society must be broken, but often the network of reciprocal obligations are so strong that the individual is either unwilling or unable to break away.[12]

This seems particularly true of Europe, where blue-collar workers have shown little desire to pursue higher class status gains. In Holland, for example, studies have shown that the Dutch workers enjoyed far greater affluence in the 1960s but that aspirations in this period still remained very limited. The working class clearly did not indulge in invidious comparisons with the income or social position of other groups and there was also very little evidence of occupational aspirations—i.e. a wish to make career advances.[13]

It has been argued that this slow pace in acquiring middle class symbols of consumption suggests a lack of incentive to advance in status and testifies to the persistence of a ceiling to working class goals and horizons. There was also found to be (in England more particularly) 'a peculiar mistrust of "those at the top", a feeling of being passive objects in the upper classes' struggle which led to a retreat to the realm of leisure and television'.[14]

The evidence of American blue-collar attitudes to middle class values and to status and prestige considerations confirms the European experience, although to a far lesser extent. Overall, it would appear that status directed consumption offers no real attraction to working classes in general. Possibly the greatest temptation to conspicuously consume is given to those skilled working class members whose income may be such that it gives them the opportunity to distance themselves socially from their class peers. However, the evidence here suggests that status conscious individuals within this sub-group are often more concerned to ensure that their children are able to 'move up a class'. To this end, they find it preferable to invest in education rather than in short term economic display which offers no long term prospect of social advancement in their eyes.[15]

There is substantial evidence to show that the working classes in both America and Europe have increased their expenditures dramatically in recent, more affluent years. At the same time, very little of this increased spending has been identified as status directed conspicuous consumption and a considerable caution in interpreting any expenditure as such has been continually stressed by researchers:

> In those instances where blue-collar workers at least appear to have adopted features of a middle class life-style, care must be taken to differentiate between the behavioural or consumption pattern and the meaning attached to it by the actors involved. Thus buying a home or a colour television, or having friends round to 'dinner', are all activities that superficially could be described as middle class. And yet the data indicates that this is not the case. Rather, they can be viewed simply as extensions of established behavioural patterns made possible by factors such as affluence or improved occupational conditions.[16]

Given the predominantly middle class, white collar preoccupation with conspicuous consumption, how significant a feature of buyer behaviour can it be considered to be? With respect to the occupational and educational elites, there are some grounds for believing that they may for the most part be reluctant conspicuous consumers. Some observers have argued that there is little or no evidence to suggest that the emergent middle classes either admired or sought to emulate the high levels of conspicuous consumption which were adopted by the new industrial elites of the late nineteenth century. It has been claimed that the twentieth century meritocrats developed their own status symbols quite independently of the preferences of the more traditional elites, and the notion that the process of influence is a vertical one which moves downwards from higher status groups—thus encouraging 'pecuniary emulation'—has not found universal acceptance.[17]

It may well be the case that the middle classes have no innate desire to conspicuously consume but the reality of their situation requires them to display income and wealth in order to establish claim to the status afforded to the meritocratic elite. General observation is sufficient to confirm that the educationally and occupationally privileged display their social standing through adopting appropriately 'conspicuous' expenditure patterns. However, it is still possible to concede that, other things being equal, such consumption may be reluctantly undertaken.

With regard to the lower middle classes and their social aspirations, the act of ostentatious economic display is both a necessity and an approved activity which has to be legitimised, in their eyes, as a proper way to secure status gains. Whilst conspicuous consumption may be disliked per se, it has to be undertaken and defended by those who are status sensitive enough to be motivated by considerations of social prestige and advancement. And the 'vertical' element in lower middle class conspicuous expenditure—which would appear to run counter to the 'horizontal strata' theory of social relationships in affluent societies—is more apparent than real, for although the act of conspicuous consumption appears vertically motivated to the outside observer, the consumer sees himself as a member of the broad middle classes and not of any lower socio-economic grouping and therefore believes the consumption to be motivated by within-group and not between-group competition for status.

The argument that no individual happily spends significant amounts of money in order to make status gains is attractive on purely rational grounds. However, it does not in any way reduce the individual's need for conspicuous consumption in a social system which may theoretically reject such display but which is almost inevitably imperfectly organised and can not remove the effectiveness of money and wealth display as an efficient way to achieve social status. We can therefore still expect considerable levels of ostentatious economic display within consumer societies which are other-directed yet 'horizontal' in terms of social relationships.

The relative degree of conspicuous consumption undertaken by the diploma and administrative elites on the one hand and the lower middle class white-collar groups on the other will be primarily determined by the levels of discretionary income enjoyed by the two groups.[18] It has been argued that narrowing income differentials have significantly reduced the financial distinctions which can be drawn between the two groups, thus contributing to an 'emerging classlessness'. Whilst it is undoubtedly true that the income gap between the middle and working classes has narrowed quite significantly in the affluent societies as the balance of industrial and economic power has changed,[19] the weight of evidence suggests that the economic distinctions within the broad middle class itself are still quite clear and that, contrary to widespread belief, the economic status of the educational elites compared with that of the lower middle class groups is still relatively privileged.[20] Although an overlap has always existed between middle and lower middle groups (social boundaries never being finely drawn) the former still appear to do considerably better financially.

The continuing earnings gap gives the 'upper' middle class the advantage in terms of opportunity to conspicuously consume and this advantage is increased because of another important, longer term distinction which has to be made between the two groups. For whilst the diploma elites normally have a clearly structured career plan which ensures them of a steady increase in real salary over their working life, the lower middle class, typified by clerks and supervisory workers, can look forward to far less financial progress—indeed their earnings (in real terms) may peak or plateau in their mid-twenties. The educated upper middle class may well live alongside lower level white-collar workers in the early part of their career and may at that time enjoy roughly the same income, but the two groups are nevertheless vastly different in terms of potential earning power—a fact that in turn has important implications with respect to spending power:

> The executive trainee's family can, with some safety, live in a style beyond its present means, because it knows that, unless the breadwinner is notably incompetent, a series of automatic raises lie ahead. The white-collar family next door, making the same income but with few likely raises ahead, often strains to keep pace with the high-living neighbour.[21]

Other things being equal, therefore, the opportunity to conspicuously consume lies far more with the upper middle class group from whom we should expect to see a significantly high level of ostentatious display. The two factors mentioned above—lower absolute incomes and a reduced expectation of incomes growth—would clearly act as constraints on lower middle class economic behaviour. However, general observation will quickly establish that these lower socio-economic groups can and do conspicuously consume on a highly significant scale and that the theoretical income and expectations constraints on such behaviour are often entirely absent in practice. To understand how this is made possible, it is now necessary to broaden the analysis and to examine the structure and imperatives of the modern consumer oriented society, identifying why and how both governments and the business world have felt impelled to ensure that constraints on conspicuous consumption at all levels of society are reduced to a level compatible with social, economic and industrial needs.

Affluent societies have very high levels of capital stock accumulation and a productive capacity which can only be sustained and made profitable if demand for goods and services runs at a level high enough to justify mass production and volume output into the distribution system. Efficient production is dependent on the overall level of demand for the products that existing resources are capable of manufacturing and also on the potential demand for new products which will encourage additional investment in new productive capacity.

To some considerable extent, the broad redistribution of wealth and the greater levels of discretionary income enjoyed by the population as a whole ensures a basic (high) level of demand for many commodities but the momentum of demand has to be maintained and overall consumption levels improved whenever and wherever possible. Failure to maintain an adequate flow of goods and services into the economy results not only in falling profitability within the private sector of industry but also leaves government without the necessary growth in financial resources to maintain, improve and expand the operation of public sector services.

In seeking to maximise consumer demand for goods and services, however, manufacturers and governments are made increasingly aware that 'want creation' must come to play a far more critical and important role than is the case in a less developed economic system. In affluent societies, income levels are high enough to ensure that basic, primary needs are quickly and easily satisfied and that a considerable amount of discretionary income will be available to the individual consumer. Having met physiological needs, however, the only significant opportunity for major expansion of consumer demand lies in encouraging and catering to the secondary or psychological desires of people—desires which for the most part are conditioned and stimulated by the individual's social environment. It follows, therefore, that demand creation comes to rely heavily on the ability and willingness of producers to expand product sales (and so improve overall micro and macro profitability) by themselves stimulating the level of social wants.

The industrial, commercial and technological infrastructure of consumer oriented societies is particularly geared to creating and exploiting psychologically and sociologically grounded demand. Firstly, the sophisticated mass communication networks provide the mechanism through which ideas, opinions, social values and trends (whether real or 'manufactured') can be transmitted. Secondly, a highly effective advertising industry is able to research in depth into specific social and socio-economic motivations and to subsequently promote products in such a way that their psychological 'benefits' are most apparent. Finally, modern systems of retail distribution are available to promote and merchandise goods in a variety of socially effective ways.

In seeking to maximise consumer demand, producers and their advertising agencies come to be particularly aware of the very strong status considerations which can influence the purchase of many commodities. The levels of prestige and social acceptance given to particular products are of especial interest to status sensitive groups and it is in the interests of manufacturers of socially 'visible' products to lay heavy emphasis on the real or imagined status of their products if they wish to find the widest possible sale within a particular market.

115

It has already been argued that status sensitivity is particularly great for two groups which can be broadly placed within the middle class of affluent societies and this significant level of concern with social standing and prestige can clearly be used to considerable advantage by those who seek to supply these markets. At the same time, it is not in the interests of producers seeking volume sales of a particular product to attempt to segment this middle class market and to separate out the two competing status groups. A marketing policy which effectively discriminates between two broadly compatible status motivated groups is counterproductive to the mass producer. Rather, sales of a particular status directed commodity will be maximised if the product in question appeals not only to the members of a specific socio-economic or reference group but also to those who, for whatever reasons, aspire to membership of such groups. Given the need for volume turnover (and this is an essential precondition) the manufacturer cannot afford to screen potential purchasers according to their real, imagined or aspired social position: on the contrary, he must seek to sell to the broadest possible market and to minimise the social distinctions between all those who, on status motivated grounds, can be considered potential buyers.

To do this, marketing strategy has therefore not only to reassure those wishing to reveal their existing membership of a higher social group that the product in question is of a quality level acceptable for conspicuous display within the group, but also to persuade or 'educate' those potential purchasers who aspire to the same social group that the purchase of the product does indeed reveal consumer taste and will be acceptable to the aspirant group. In order to achieve both these objectives, the seller must, in part, concentrate his efforts on breaking down any barriers to product evaluation and preference which can result from occupational and educational differences between potential consumers.

The differences within the broad middle class with which manufacturers of socially visible status goods are most concerned have already been described. Firstly, there may exist, in theory perhaps but also in the minds of actual and potential consumers, a barrier of 'revealed taste' which could deter aspirant groups from conspicuously consuming products whose social value is uncertain to them. This barrier is, however, easily overcome when producers take advantage of the comprehensive communications network either to transmit known values across socio-economic divides and within particular groups or adopt advertising and promotional programmes which effectively seek to dictate taste at the appropriate social levels. Whilst the niceties of social behaviour may not be 'transferable', consumption behaviour can be more easily taught and learnt.

Secondly, there is the income and income expectations barrier already mentioned—a barrier which again works to the advantage of the higher, more economically privileged group and which could be most effective in reducing the propensity to conspicuously consume at lower social levels. Whilst taste is intangible and can be readily transmitted or manipulated, the very tangible reality of limitations on discretionary income is not directly within the power of the producer to change. However, the consumer oriented society—with its dependence on high levels of production and demand—has a particular interest in reducing this income constraint to a minimum, not least because, as has been argued, individuals believe that standards of consumption most eloquently reveal differences in income and therefore in social standing and achievement. The circular relationship between consumption, income and prestige, and the central importance of this relationship to status beliefs and status theory, can be summarised:

> Prestige goes to successful people and success in society is closely correlated with income. Once a group of high income people are recognised as a group of superior status, their consumption standard itself becomes one of the criteria for judging success. Since almost any consumption theory is consistent with the view that high-income families will spend more on consumption than low-income families: high standards of consumption become established as a criteria for high status. Once this has occurred it becomes difficult for anyone to attain a high status position unless he can maintain a high consumption standard, regardless of any other qualifications he may have.[22]

The status seeking individual who aspires to membership of a higher socio-economic group will therefore be determined to adopt a consumption pattern which, as far as is possible, will not reveal any relative income inferiority. This could clearly work against conspicuous consumption in that the level of ostentatious display which can be achieved on a limited income may not be sufficient to avoid unfavourable comparisons with others who may enjoy a substantially higher level of discretionary income. A possible reaction to this threat is of course for individuals to reduce or eliminate their attempts to be conspicuous in their consumption behaviour—an option which would be particularly unwelcome to producers of status related products of a potentially high sales value.

From the producers' point of view, the incomes constraint on conspicuous expenditure needs to be minimised. To this end, a major development in the affluent societies has been the considerable expansion of credit and hire-purchase facilities which are intended in part to allow income limited individuals access to additional funds with which to make purchases they could not otherwise at that time afford. The growth of credit linked consumption has been one of the more remarkable developments in the consumer societies which have come into being on both sides of the Atlantic. In effectively increasing present income by allowing individuals to discount future earnings, the potential market for conspicuous, status linked products is significantly expanded—the more so when the promise of continued future credit support allows individuals to believe that the risks associated with current overspending are substantially reduced.

Companies whose products are designed and promoted either wholly or partially as status goods are today heavily committed to expanding sales and market opportunities by encouraging the use of credit amongst those customers who would otherwise find it difficult to buy their products on cash terms. In pursuing such policies, however, they have needed—and obtained—the support of two important allies.

Firstly, the development of credit business has been backed by many financial institutions who have been happy to see a substantial proportion of their assets underpinning credit sales of manufactured goods and services by making funds available at highly profitable rates of interest. Bank credit facilities have been heavily promoted in more recent years and the level of credit card usage bears witness to the success of the banks in persuading consumers that the conspicuous symbols of social and economic success are now available for immediate consumption. And whilst interest payments on credit accounts are often known by consumers to be very high, there has been little evidence that this knowledge has in any way served to diminish the willingness of individuals to carry a substantial level of credit based debt in order to satisfy their immediate needs.

In addition to the support given to credit sales by the major banks and other financial institutions, a further stimulus has come from retailers who have also seen the development to be in their own best interests and who have co-operated with manufacturers and finance houses in promoting such sales. By definition, a majority of conspicuous status linked products are on offer at equally 'conspicuous' prices which, in the absence of credit facilities, would discourage many potential buyers in the limited income groups. By financing sales through charge accounts or through instalment credit, retailers have found it possible to increase demand for status goods by a significant amount and have therefore continued to expand the scale of their credit linked business. Indeed, in more recent years, the larger retailers have moved further and have increased their commitment by issuing and financing their own credit card operations as a means of encouraging store loyalty and repeat purchasing among their customers.

The alliance of manufacturers, financiers and retailers in expanding markets and increasing long term corporate profitability by developing credit based demand has undoubtedly been successful. Consumers have been persuaded to modify perceptions of their buying power and this has certainly reduced the significance of current income as a constraint on consumption. This success has also more recently been given added stimulus by the particularly high levels of inflation which have been much in evidence in the majority of affluent Western societies and which have had the effect of encouraging individuals to 'buy now, pay later' in order to take advantage of rapidly falling real money values. However, in recognising the success of credit based demand management, certain serious limitations on the effectiveness of credit as a means of expanding sales of conspicuous, socially visible status goods have to be acknowledged.

Firstly, notwithstanding the greater overall acceptance of the use of credit, research suggests that income related values remain the most important factors in deciding whether consumers purchase or do not purchase a particular commodity. There is also good evidence to show that as income plays a more dominant role the more expensive is the product or product group under consideration. Given that the pure conspicuous consumer is necessarily more interested in relatively high priced goods, then the income related perceptions of what can and can not be afforded remain very significant and the 'credit effect' on conspicuous consumption is correspondingly diminished.

Secondly, although the advantages and opportunities afforded by the use of credit have been heavily promoted, significant groups of consumers have remained strongly opposed to credit buying—for many social, religious and cultural reasons—and have resisted most attempts to change their buying habits. For these consumers, status goods continue to be purchased—if at all—out of savings and the greater availability of credit prompts little additional spending. Whilst many observers see such resistance to the 'credit culture' as a relatively short term phenomenon which will eventually disappear, it is still much in evidence among a minority of buyers in modern, consumer based affluent societies.

Thirdly, the very existence and availability of credit for the purchase of conspicuous goods has the effect of diminishing the perceived status value of these goods in so far as the conspicuous consumer is concerned—for in easing the price and payments burden such products are put within the reach of many new buyers, thus reducing their ability to impress others when purchased or consumed. Consequently, whilst credit sales of conspicuous products may increase by such goods being made available to more potential buyers, they are partially offset by a fall in demand amongst those conspicuous consumers who are not income limited at the cash asking price but who find the products' status value much reduced by their increased availability.

Finally, it is necessary to recognise that the management of credit is today not only a corporate but a political matter. Governments reserve the right to intervene in the market to control both the availability of credit and the terms on which credit is offered and politicians, as guardians of the social conscience, often seek to impose restrictions in those areas of consumption which may be considered either socially divisive or wasteful. In this context, demand for status goods generates little political sympathy and credit facilities for the purchase of such 'luxury' products are often curtailed by statute—a policy which effectively undermines attempts by manufacturers and retailers to expand sales.

The above constraints on spending show that the development of extended credit facilities has a significant but limited usefulness with respect to status goods and that the core problem of consumers' limited discretionary incomes remains very real for those wishing to promote conspicuous products. Recognising the limitations of credit policies, and given their inability to attack the 'per capita' income constraint directly, many manufacturers have adopted an alternative marketing strategy which seeks to reduce the importance of personal income and credit availability by changing consumer perceptions of status value in the products they buy.

The barriers created by low income and by the limited effectiveness of credit expansion are only critical for as long as price alone is able to determine a product's social worth for the conspicuous consumer. Under conditions of pure conspicuous consumption, financial constraints on the level of purchases are absolute in that the consumer recognises only the (high) price of products as indicative of their quality or social value. Manufacturers and retailers have realised, however, that if they can break the monopoly of price as a quality indicator then the financial barriers to sales are substantially reduced. To this end, they have made efforts to promote a new form of status consumption intended to reduce the role of price as the prime indicator of status value. Emphasis is increasingly placed on other variables such as quality in use (i.e. utility in the classical sense) and on 'taste'. The acceptability of products is strongly associated, through appropriate advertising campaigns, with factors which effectively diminish the central position of product price in establishing social prestige. And advertising agencies have undoubtedly met with considerable success in implementing this policy—a policy designed, in essence, to reach and retain those consumers who would otherwise not be in the market for conspicuous status goods because of income limitations or because credit facilities prove to be either too restricted or are seen as culturally or financially unacceptable.

Volume manufacturers of 'visible' products, therefore, have broadly adopted three interdependent strategies as far as the potential demand for conspicuous goods is concerned. Firstly, they have seen no merit in segmenting customers within the broad middle class who, whilst enjoying different levels of wealth, income and income expectations, nevertheless do share one common overriding objective—that of status advance, consolidation and reinforcement. And the problem of income limitations on consumer spending has been tackled in two ways—firstly by seeking

to increase funds available to the individual by the extension and promotion of credit buying and secondly by playing down the importance
of price in conspicuous consumption decisions, a policy which, when
successful, effectively reduces the problem of revealed income inferiority.

For these strategies to be successful, the producer is dependent on a
highly efficient system of communication which is able to cross real or
apparent socio-economic barriers, on public acceptance of credit buying
and finally on establishing surrogates for price which are able to retain
roughly the same levels of social 'cachet'. In all three areas, the pattern
of economic, social and technological change in affluent societies is
favourable. Firstly, the advent of television and the substantial expansion
of all media activities ensures that status sensitive individuals are kept
informed—or persuaded—of the social and economic preferences of all
groups. Secondly, there is a vigorous development and social acceptance
of the use of credit as an aid to consumption; and finally, the advertising
industry is able to redirect buyers' attention away from product price
and towards other status related factors which are taken by many consumers as acceptable, conspicuous price substitutes.

Advertising in particular has come to play a most important role in
reshaping the pattern of conspicuous consumption. The visual impact
of television is such that advertisers have been able to 'place' their client's
products in a socio-economic context appropriate to status sensitive
markets and they have been most effective in so doing. Regardless of
the reality of product acceptability at different social levels, product
image in the consumer oriented societies is to a very great extent a
controlled variable and producers have been quick to see the vast potential of locating their products within the right (if 'mythical') socio-
economic environment. The management of atmospherics has become
an important aspect of product planning and this is especially true of
socially 'visible' products directed at potential conspicuous consumers.

The attraction and importance of high price is often understated in
advertisements and is replaced with claims that social prestige comes
from being seen to consume products of quality which are recognised as
such by status sensitive social groups. Success or failure is decided by
the relative effectiveness with which socially visible products are
'positioned' in the actual or potential consumers' minds but the continuing high levels of advertising expenditures which are concerned with
the social engineering of prestige products bear witness to the relevance
and profitability of such activity.

The success of advertising and promotional campaigns directed at
increasing the conspicuous consumption of any particular product has
been positively influenced by parallel changes in the system of distribution for such goods. The importance of selecting the correct channel of
distribution is fundamental to the marketing and promotion of conspicuous products; indeed, it can be argued that the conditions under

which status products are bought are perhaps as important to the conspicuous consumer as the real or imagined social attributes of the actual product which is to be purchased. In marketing such goods, therefore, the most successful stores and retail outlets are normally those which deliberately develop a clear-cut image conveying a particular socio-economic status and contrive to make potential customers who do not 'belong' feel as uncomfortable as possible.[23]

The act of purchase or of shopping is an additional source of status satisfaction in so far that 'being seen' at a prestige store enhances the status of the shopper and vice versa. Again, atmosphere comes to play a critical role in influencing the customer's opinion of a particular product, for the successful positioning of a status good—achieved for the most part through effective advertising—needs to be reinforced by the conditions under which the product is then offered for sale. The distribution channel—i.e. the retail outlet—can seek to cater quite explicitly to the status requirements of its customers and can project a store image which is complementary—in symbolic terms—to the prestige products which are being sold.

To secure this correct store image, distributors attempt to ensure that retail advertising corresponds to the character of the store projected through its personnel, terms of business and general atmosphere. Store personality and product prestige are often seen as so interdependent that many manufacturers of socially visible status products directed specifically at conspicuous consumers adopt a policy of exclusive or selective distribution to ensure that product 'image' is generated not only through appropriate promotional strategies but also through the transaction process itself.

Finally, producers can not be satisfied with a pattern of conspicuous consumption which ensures demand for status linked products but which does not generate demand for such goods at a repurchase rate sufficient to justify and maintain volume production. Here again, technology and the advertising industry work together to produce an acceptable level of repeat business by seeking to shorten the conspicuous 'life' of socially visible products. Planned obsolescence ensures that goods bought for ostentatious display possess high status attributes for only a short period of time and are rapidly outdated by later more 'sophisticated' versions in the same product class. Rather than seek material or functional obsolescence, however, suppliers of conspicuous goods are more immediately concerned with securing an acceptable rate of 'social obsolescence' by making products quickly unfashionable.[24] To do this, heavy emphasis is placed on product attributes such as style and ornamentation (i.e. the visual attributes) as this causes the consumer to become preoccupied with appearances rather than with functional utility of any sort. Changes in style can often be secured quite simply, perhaps by changes in colour[25] or by design changes which, although superficial in themselves, are able to create significant visual differences between old and new product versions.[26]

To generate an acceptably high rate of change in the ranking of socially approved products, producers and their advertisers are faced with the problem of convincing their various publics that new product versions are socially superior to the old and are therefore important, even essential, purchases if status is to be reinforced or status aspirations are to be realised. To do this, they may elect to identify opinion leaders in the particular status groups they wish to influence and to use these individuals to establish new ideas and attitudes at the top of the status hierarchy. Theoretically, these new values and beliefs should then 'trickle down' to all other members of the reference or social class group and eventually to those who aspire to join these groups. A second alternative is to discount the importance of individual opinion leaders and to concentrate promotional efforts on all members and aspiring members of a particular group or class in the belief that opinion change is generated not by a cumulative build up of converts reacting to status superiors but by a groundswell change in values generated in the body of the group—a change which quickly influences the accepted norms and rankings of the group as a whole.

Irrespective of the approach adopted by the individual firm—and there is evidence which would appear to support and justify the use of both strategies—the fact remains that the social obsolescence of products is increasingly created by agencies external to the social class or group in question—agencies which have a commitment only to securing the best possible repurchase and replacement rate for the products of their clients.

There can be no doubt that the promotion of socially conspicuous, mass produced goods through selective product planning, advertising, pricing and distribution policies has been highly successful in generating the level of business needed by volume producers in the affluent societies. The broad middle class, which in essence contains the great majority of conspicuous consumers, has certainly been persuaded to purchase goods which have been promoted and sold as status symbols. At both a theoretical and a practical level there should be nothing surprising in this outcome, for the central assumption made by the producers—i.e. that a general standard or scale can be established against which products are measured for their social value—is supported, in theory and empirically, by the conclusion that a 'demonstration effect' exists in so far as conspicuously visible products are concerned.[27]

It is argued that consumer preferences, particularly of socially visible goods of a high prestige value, are not independent of the economic behaviour of others but are in fact interdependent; that social needs can be satisfied by any of a number of qualitatively different types of goods; that these different types of goods or, in the broader sense, ways of doing things, are regarded as superior or inferior to one another; and that there is a generally agreed upon scale of ranks for the goods which can be used for any specific purpose.[28] More simply, if 'society' decides that one particular good is socially superior to another, the consumer can be expected to adjust his own preferences and buying behaviour in favour of the approved commodity. The only precondition is that the potential consumer is in fact informed—or has direct knowledge—of the ranking generally given to the product or products in question.[29]

The demonstration effect—sometimes referred to as the 'bandwagon effect'—supports the producers' belief that products can be established as socially desirable with one group or class in the expectation that its subsequent high ranking within that group will be made known to other (lower) socio-economic groups who are highly motivated to make status gains—the lower middle class for example—and will subsequently ensure volume sales of the product in question across two or more socio-economic sectors. It also lends credibility to the argument that status sensitive groups belonging to the same broadly defined middle class can be treated as a single market in the expectation that views and values will easily be transmitted across and between sub-groups and will generate a volume level of sales for those products which are successful in securing a prestige 'ranking' on the social scale.

Whilst the demonstration effect—derived indirectly from behavioural theories of opinion leadership and group attitude formation—can offer an explanation of the overall level of conspicuous consumption, it does not afford a greater insight into the actual (as opposed to the assumed) motives which determine the conspicuous purchase decisions of middle and lower middle class consumers. The bandwagon effect argues that volume demand is generated entirely by individuals wishing to 'follow the crowd'—i.e. to conform socially—but this is an unacceptable generalisation in so far as any detailed study of conspicuous consumption is concerned. In many ways it is more important to know how and why these individuals emulate the behaviour of others and in which ways their product preferences are formed, given the efforts of producers to generate volume sales. That status motivated volume consumption is much in evidence in the affluent societies is not in doubt. However, producers in practice employ not one but many strategies in seeking to secure high turnover for their products and it is important to know which of the theoretical assumptions on which these strategies are based are in fact shown to be of substance. If such post-purchase analyses can be made, then it is possible to elaborate and expand on the concept of the demonstration effect by identifying more precisely those socio-economic 'appeals' and advertising policies which are most successful in generating volume sales of conspicuous goods in the consumer oriented societies. This in turn tells us more about the nature and direction of mass market conspicuous consumption behaviour.

It has already been noted that little research has been carried out directly into the motivations and purchase preferences of conspicuous consumers. Evidence of status linked consumer behaviour is only indirectly available—that is, it tends to occur in research studies which were set up to examine entirely different aspects of product choice and buyer behaviour but which coincidentally produce information which is of value to the conspicuous consumption researcher. Again, the principal reason why specific studies into conspicuous consumption have been particularly difficult to design and carry out has been the entirely rational and understandable reluctance of consumers to admit that any purchases are motivated by personal status considerations.

Notwithstanding the paucity of direct research work, there are now some good indicators available of the way in which consumers have reacted to the manufacture, advertising and marketing of conspicuous goods. Firstly, with regard to the assumptions made by producers concerning the motivation or stimuli to conspicuous consumption, there is now much evidence to show that people are particularly influenced in their consumption behaviour by the social environment in which they live. Cultural values seem to correlate significantly with consumer behaviour in so far as 'visible' products are concerned. Group cohesiveness is high and similarity of brand choice—i.e. the demonstration effect seems to be primarily conditioned by a consumer's family, his peers and by 'significant reference groups'.[30]

In particular, the evidence for horizontal (within-group) reference would appear to be strong. There is a special importance attached to the opinion of small primary groups and it has been demonstrated experimentally that product choice is strongly influenced, perhaps dominated, by an individual's immediate need to conform and react to small face-to-face groups.[31]

The strength of horizontal reference could indicate that there is little incentive or desire for individuals to seek or achieve vertical status gains and would seem to support those who have argued strongly that within-group relationships in the consumer oriented societies are so important that between-group 'vertical' stimuli can be safely discounted.[32] However there is also evidence which confirms that 'socially distant' aspiration reference groups—that is, groups lying some considerable socio-economic distance from the consumer—may also at times have a significant impact on consumer behaviour and provide a vertical incentive to conspicuously consume.[33]

In seeking to establish the relative importance of within-group and between-group goals, we can refer to research which has been carried out on the influence of 'real self-image' and 'ideal self-image' consumption patterns. A recognition of real or true self-image can be taken to imply a corresponding preoccupation with horizontal within-group status whilst concern for ideal self-image can be considered more likely to reflect the interests of those who are primarily motivated by vertical status gains.

Research evidence of the relative importance of real and ideal self-images on conspicuous purchase decisions suggests that it is in fact necessary to distinguish between product preference and product consumption. Most tests support the contention that both concepts of self can be influential in the preference/consumption process but show a clear demarcation between the relative areas of influence. Experiments directed at exploring the preference patterns of socially visible goods have shown that preferred brands are often more congruent with ideal self rather than with true self.[34] In contrast, actual product purchase and consumption is often far more closely aligned with real self-image.[35] This distinction between preference and consumption is most easily explained when the income constraint on product choice is introduced into the analysis; limited income can clearly compel individuals to differentiate between what they would like to buy and what they are able to buy.[36]

Similarly, with store preference, whilst consumers prefer certain stores as being most congruent with their ideal self-image, they tend to patronise shops whose characteristics are congruent with their real self-image.[37] This is perhaps explained not only by income and wealth constraints but also by the wish of consumers not to place themselves in a position of 'social risk' and possible loss of face by moving outside what they know to be their real socio-economic environment.[38] In any event, we can reasonably accept the proposition that there is distinction to be made—both in terms of product choice and in store patronage—between preferred and actual purchase and consumption behaviour.

Other research suggests that conspicuous consumers may in fact be more defensive in their behaviour than theories of status and prestige incentive would allow. Ostentatious display has traditionally been taken to be an aggressive or offensive form of consumer behaviour directed at securing a particular status goal. However, in selecting socially conspicuous products, individuals may not concentrate on 'most preferred' goods but be more concerned with avoiding products which would not be acceptable to particular reference groups.[39] Again, for products of high social risk, status sensitive individuals sometimes appear to be less interested in shopping at a store of particularly high status and more concerned with not shopping at a retail outlet which may prove to be socially unacceptable.[40] If such defensive behaviour is indeed commonplace, then it suggests that the ranking system of product acceptability which is a part of the demonstration effect is of importance to the consumer not in establishing a list of approved products but in isolating socially 'bad' products which he or she can then avoid.

Overall, the pattern of consumption which emerges from the empirical studies which have directly or indirectly provided information on conspicuous consumption suggests that while volume sales have indeed resulted from the promotion of status linked products, motivation to purchase may to some extent have been misunderstood or misinterpreted by producers. Firstly, it would appear that the influence of television and other media in persuading people to buy socially conspicuous goods may only be significant when the potential buyer is assured of the fact that his immediate social contacts would approve of the product's acquisition and consumption. Most empirical research emphasises the importance to consumers of ensuring conformity to family and small group expectations in their product purchases. Secondly, consumers seem to be far more cautious in terms of self-image than may be supposed by those who seek to promote goods on the basis of the potential vertical status gains they offer. Real rather than ideal self-image appears to dominate the decision to purchase socially visible goods. Finally, and possibly as a consequence of the above two considerations, conspicuous consumers may at times be motivated more strongly by the possibility of minimising the social risk associated with purchases rather than by maximising the potential status gains.

These preliminary conclusions suggest that volume market conspicuous consumption is horizontally rather than vertically directed and appears to be motivated more by a desire to conform than to make significant status advances. If this is so, it also suggests that manufacturers who have consolidated volume sales of their products to the mass market have been successful not in motivating people to raise their socio-economic aspirations but in breaking down occupational, educational and financial barriers within the broad middle class markets in which they operate.

In summary: manufacturers have been successful in overcoming the information and income limitations of the many potential conspicuous consumers who are an essential part of any volume market for status linked products. The demonstration effect has worked to ensure the subsequent volume sales that have resulted. However, on the basis of the admittedly limited, and often indirect, post-purchase research evidence at present available, the market would appear to be perhaps more rational and conservative than 'earlier' patterns of conspicuous consumption (e.g. those in evidence in achieving societies) would lead us to suppose.

It has been argued that volume producers are particularly concerned with 'adapting' the phenomenon of conspicuous consumption to their own needs by firstly seeking to dilute the importance of limited availability and exclusive ownership and secondly of price as the only recognised determinant of a conspicuous product's social 'worth'. The fact that the strategy has clearly been pursued for many years in the affluent societies and has been the subject of considerable debate and controversy which has persisted over some two decades bears witness to its impact and success in generating volume demand for socially sensitive products.[41] However, there has at the same time been a reaction to the mass merchandising of conspicuous products which has created an entirely separate market for prestige goods quite distinct from that supplied by the volume manufacturers.

Notwithstanding the efforts of mass producers to restructure and control the demand for conspicuous products, the 'traditional' values associated with conspicuous consumption survive the transition from achievement to affluence. The mass produced products seen as essential to the growth and development of mature economic societies often hold little or no attraction for many socially aware consumers and there is evidence that the 'bandwagon effect' which provides the cornerstone of volume demand for conspicuous goods in turn produces a reaction—the 'snob effect'—which actively works against the interests of the mass producer. This snob effect is in evidence when status sensitive consumers come to reject a particular product as and when it is seen to be consumed by the general mass of people—the overall lack of exclusivity in consumption making the product appear 'common' in social terms, so reducing its value as an item of conspicuous display. Bandwagon and snob effects are therefore directly related; the higher the level of product consumption as a result of the bandwagon effect then the greater the snob effect can be expected to be.

'Snob' consumers can be seen as themselves comprising a separate market for conspicuous goods. Although prepared to accept the consequences of the bandwagon or demonstration effect up to a point, they increasingly turn against a product as its sales reach what is to them a socially unacceptable level. Too great a 'dilution' of the product in terms of availability and consumption produces a negative revaluation of the social worth of the commodity and an increasing resistance to purchase.

The rejection of heavily promoted mass merchandised products effectively creates a different market for conspicuously consumed goods—a market in which consumers seek to buy products whose limited availability and consumption ensures a measure of social exclusiveness. Whilst this market offers little opportunity for exploitation by volume dependent producers[42] it is ideally suited to those firms geared to small scale operations who have a limited need for sales volume, often require higher than average product mark-ups to offset the high unit cost structure of their operations and are able to manufacture highly differentiated products to order or in limited quantities.

In essence, the snob effect creates a type of demand for conspicuous goods which most nearly approximates to the classical forms of conspicuous consumption seen in the achieving societies. It is a market which is reserved for those who have the financial resources at their disposal to be able to meet prices which can appear to be excessive or extravagant but which bestow a clear 'superiority' of wealth on those seen to be consuming the product or products in question. By definition, it can never become a volume market because product price must always be set at a level which excludes (or deters) the great majority of potential consumers, thus preserving the single greatest attribute of the product in question—i.e. its ability to be consumed only by the select few who are willing and able to meet the asking price.

Unlike the very limited demand for conspicuous products in developing societies—which are not geared to mass production and in which the distribution of income and wealth is significantly unequal—the snob market for goods is not the exclusive preserve of the very rich in affluent societies. Given a limited income or limited total wealth, the individual is at liberty to arrange his discretionary expenditures in any way he sees fit. He may, for example, choose to devote a higher than average part of his resources to one particular set of purchases because he is in fact a snob in so far as those products are concerned and wishes to make purchases which effectively differentiate him from the great majority of buyers. The 'snob effect' can therefore apply to products as far apart— in price and in application—as perfume, clothes, foodstuffs, prestige furs and motor cars.

The nature of demand for high price, limited consumption commodities is clearly quite distinct from that cultivated and exploited so effectively by volume producers in the consumer oriented societies. It is therefore in the interests of manufacturers seeking to supply these markets to ensure that their own product strategy is properly geared to the preferences of the consumers they wish to serve. The overriding need is to establish the snob value of the product or products in question and to ensure that they continue to be seen as products which are certainly not manufactured for the volume market. In this end, manufacturers often adopt policies which stress rather than play down high price and selective availability and consumption. Channels of distribution are limited and often exclusive; promotional activities (i.e. below the line advertising) are never used; and advertising messages stress most particularly that the product is not intended for mass (or 'common') consumption.

The snob market therefore generates demand for products which is met for the most part by craftsmen and smaller companies who are able to exploit the quality, exclusiveness, high price and limited distribution of the goods they manufacture. Although responsible for only a small part of total industrial activity, this traditional market has become well established (and often highly profitable) in the consumer societies and is able to co-exist with the volume market for socially visible products. In many ways, the two markets are complementary and mutually supportive. Too high a level of output and demand in the volume sector can be directly responsible for increasing the importance of the snob effect and for channelling extra demand to the traditional sector whilst at the same time bringing the volume market back into equilibrium. Conversely, too great an expansion of traditional market activity—resulting perhaps in greater demand at reduced prices—will tend to shift many consumers into the volume market as product and price differentiation between the two sectors becomes more blurred.

For some considerable time it was believed that conspicuous consumption would disappear in the affluent societies as it became increasingly anachronistic, politically unacceptable and therefore self-defeating. The success which had been enjoyed by the aristocratic and industrial elites of less developed social and economic systems could not, it was argued, be repeated by adopting a policy of ostentatious economic display in societies committed to far greater equality of wealth and opportunity. However, if we can generalise on the American and European experiences of more recent years, conspicuous consumption certainly does not disappear in the post-industrial societies; rather it is 'modified' and put to use to help supply, in part, the demand for goods and services which are essential to consumer oriented welfare states committed in the main to policies of increased public benefits and full employment.

In essence, the fundamental motivation to conspicuously consume for status gain which occurs in earlier forms of social organisation is adapted to suit the radically different socio-economic structure of the modern consumer society. Firstly, pure conspicuous consumption, no longer seen as either politically or socially advantageous by the very rich and the historically privileged, is taken up by the administrative and diploma elites of the modern middle classes who see 'selective' ostentatious display as a means of status reinforcement. Secondly, the substantial redistribution of income and wealth which accompanies the changeover from achieving to affluent society produces a potential market of such size that manufacturers and their advertising agencies attempt to broaden the appeal of conspicuous consumption and to generate a substantial non-elitist (i.e. lower middle class) demand for status products which they are well able to supply.

Whilst conspicuous consumption at the very top of the social pyramid shows a relative decline, therefore, middle class bandwagon and snob effects—whether 'natural' or 'manufactured'—create markets for conspicuous, socially visible products for both the volume and the small scale producer. Limited production, specialist manufacturers find little or no need to adapt the traditional criteria of consumer product evaluation—i.e. high price and restricted distribution—but volume producers are obliged to play down the role of price and to stress the importance of social conformity and acceptance through the acquisition of socially 'approved' conspicuous products.

The social and economic inequalities of traditional and achieving societies ensured that conspicuous consumption was a privilege afforded for the most part only to those of very great ascribed or achieved wealth. In contrast, the opportunity to conspicuously consume in the affluent, post-industrial societies has been made available to individuals at all social and economic levels. This greater opportunity is in part a natural consequence of the more equitable distribution of income and wealth, in part a result of the product policies of manufacturers who have a vested interest in exploiting any potentially lucrative market for their output.

In its affluent society role as a necessary element of consumer demand, conspicuous consumption survives the entire process of social change from traditional through achieving to consumer oriented society. In all three societies, it has been attacked either as a morally indefensible or a socially divisive activity but has confounded its critics by continuing to enjoy the confidence of consumers themselves. Having focused in this and earlier chapters on the nature and incidence of conspicuous consumption within the three basic forms of social organisation, the evolution of this exceptional form of consumer behaviour can now be seen in clearer perspective and its role and importance more properly assessed.

Notes

1   See Galbraith, J.K., *The Affluent Society,* 3rd edition, Andre Deutch, London, 1977. The term 'affluent society' was first coined by Galbraith in 1959.

2   Riesman, D., *The Lonely Crowd,* Yale University Press, New Haven, 1950. Eleventh printing, July 1964, p.21.

3   Ibid., p.26.

4   Ibid., p.123. Riesman argued that a very clear distinction could be made between conspicuous consumers in the achieving and affluent societies: 'The type of acquisitive consumer who is less concerned with building up a private hoard or hobby and more concerned with showing his possessions off with fashion seems, at first glance, other-directed in his attention. Yet, if we go back to Veblen's classic work, we can see, I think, that the consumers he describes are other-directed in appearance only. The Veblenese conspicuous consumer is seeking to fit into a role demanded of him by his station, or hoped-for station, in life; whereas the other-directed consumer seeks experiences rather than things and yearns to be guided by others rather than to dazzle them with display' (p.122).

5   See Packard, V., *The Status Seekers*, Longman, London, 1960—especially Chapter 3, 'Emerging: A Diploma Elite'.

6   Galbraith, J.K., op.cit., p.70.

7   Ibid., p.72.

8   As Galbraith (1959) pointed out: 'The professional manager or executive has taken away from the man of wealth the power that is implicit in running a business. Fifty years ago Morgan, Rockefeller, Hill, Harriman and others were the undisputed masters of the business concerns they owned, or it was indisputably in their power to become so. Their sons and grandsons still have the wealth, but with rare exceptions the power implicit in the running of the firm has passed to professionals. Nor has any equivalent new generation of owning entrepreneurs come along.'

9   Galbraith, J.K., op.cit., p.77.

10   See Martineau, P., *Motivation in Advertising*, McGraw-Hill, New York, 1957.

11   Lower middle class ambitions to erect a social barrier between themselves and the working class have become more difficult to achieve as the financial 'balance of power' has swung in favour of the latter group in the affluent societies.

12   See, for example, Warner, J. Lloyd and Abbeglen, J.C., *Big Business Leaders in America*, Harper and Bros., New York, 1955, p.193; also Whyte, W.F., 'A Slum Sex Code', *American Journal of Sociology*, vol.49, July 1943, p.24.

13   Ter Hoeven, P.J.A., *Arbeiders tussen welvaart en onvrede, Alphen aan den Rijn*, N. Samson, 1969; and Buiter, J.H., *Modern Salariaat in Wording*, Universitaire Pers., Rotterdam, 1967.

14   Katona, G., Strumpel, B. and Zahn, E., *Aspirations and Affluence*, McGraw-Hill, New York, 1971, p.35. See also, Goldthorpe, J.H. and Lockwood, D., 'Not So Bourgeois After All', *New Society*, October—December, 1962.

15   Investment in education as a way to greater family prestige again implies a belief in long term ascribed status rather than in status immediately achieved through material display.

16   Mackenzie, G., *The Aristocracy of Labour: The Position of Skilled Craftsmen in the American Class Structure*, Cambridge University Press, London, 1973.

17   See Katona, G., *The Powerful Consumer*, McGraw-Hill, New York, 1960, p.161; Riesman, D., op.cit; and Katz, E. and Lazarsfeld, P.F., *Personal Influence*, Free Press, Glencoe, Illinois, 1955.

18 Assuming an equal or near-equal motivation to conspicuously consume.

19 See Willmott, P. and Young, M., *Family and Class in a London Suburb*, Routledge and Kegan Paul, London, 1960. This study found that there had been (by 1960) a considerable narrowing of income differentials and that people in the middle and working classes were tending to spend their money on very much the same thing. Willmott and Young sensed an 'emerging classlessness' but in reality the tensions of social class were still there, i.e. the middle classes still wanted to separate themselves from the working class— 'the nearer the classes are drawn by the objective facts of income, style of life and housing, the more are middle class people liable to pull them apart' (p.122).

20 Roberts, K., Cook, F.G., Clark, S.C. and Semeonoff, E., *The Fragmentary Class Structure*, Heinemann, London, 1977. Also Routh, G., *Occupations and Pay in Great Britain, 1906–1960*, Cambridge University Press, London, 1965.

21 Packard, V., op.cit., p.224. See also Whyte, W.H., *The Organisation Man*, Simon and Schuster, New York, 1956, p.307.

22 Duesenberry, J.S., *Income, Saving and the Theory of Consumer Behavior*, Harvard University Press, Cambridge, Mass., 1949, p.30.

23 See Packard, V., op.cit., chapter 9, 'Shopping for Status'.

24 Sometimes referred to as 'planned obsolescence of desirability' or 'psychological obsolescence' (see Cheskin, L., *Why People Buy*, Liveright Publishing Co., New York, 1959).

25 Particularly the case with home furnishings and decoration, fashion clothes, etc.

26 Changes in car design as an example: many cars are visually—and therefore socially—'dated' within two years of first being produced.

27 Duesenberry, J.S., op.cit.

28 Ibid., p.22.

29 Ibid., p.27.

30 See, for example, Henry, W.A., 'Cultural Values Do Correlate with Consumer Behaviour', *Journal of Marketing Research*, May 1979, pp.121-7; Hair, J.F. (Jr) and Anderson, R.E., 'Culture, Acculturation and Consumer Behaviour', Combined Proceedings, Spring and Fall Conference, American Marketing Association, 1972, pp.423-8; Grubb, E.L. and Stern, B.L., 'Self-Concept and Significant Others', *Journal of Marketing Research*, August 1971, pp.382-5; Witt, R.E., 'Informal Social Group Influence on Consumer Brand Choice', *Journal of Marketing Research*, November 1969, pp.473-476;

Bourne, F.S., *Group Influence in Marketing and Public Relations,* in Likert, R. and Hayes, S.P. (eds) 'Some Applications of Behavioural Research', UNESCO, 1959; Venkatesan, M., 'Experimental Study of Consumer Behaviour Conformity and Independence', *Journal of Marketing Research,* November 1966; Mosch, G.P., 'Social Comparison and Informal Group Influence', *Journal of Marketing Research ,* August 1976, pp.237-44; Hempel. D.J., 'Family Buying Decisions: A Cross-Cultural Perspective', *Journal of Marketing Research,* August 1974, p.295; Cox. E.P., 'Family Purchase Decision Making and the Process of Adjustment', *Journal of Marketing Research,* May 1975, p.189.

31   Stafford, J.E., 'Effects of Group Influence on Consumer Brand Preferences', *Journal of Marketing Research,* February 1966, pp.68-74; Venkatesan, M., *Consumer Behaviour: Conformity and Independence,* in Kassarjian, H.H. and Robertson, R.T. (eds) 'Perspectives in Consumer Behaviour', Scott, Foresman, Glenview, Illinois, 1965, pp.274-5 and 306-12.

32   Katona, G., *The Powerful Consumer,* op.cit., Katz, E. and Lazarsfeld, P.F., *Personal Influence,* op.cit.

33   As, for example, Cocanougher, A.B. and Bruce, G.D., 'Socially Distant Reference Groups and Consumer Aspirations', *Journal of Marketing Research,* August 1971, pp.379-81.

34   Hughes, R.E., 'Self Concept and Brand Preference: A Partial Replication', *Journal of Business,* vol.49, 1976, pp.530-40; Birdwell, A., 'A Study of the Influence of Image Congruence on Consumer Choice', *Journal of Business,* January 1968, pp.76-88. See also Grubb, E.L. and Grathwohl, H.L., 'Consumer Self-Concept Symbolism and Market Behaviour: A Theoretical Approach', *Journal of Marketing*, vol.31, October 1967, pp.22-7.

35   Ross, I., 'Self-Concept and Brand Preference', *Journal of Business*, vol.44, June 1971, pp.38-50; Grubb, E.L. and Hupp, G., 'Perception of Self Generalised Stereotypes and Brand Selection', *Journal of Marketing Research,* February 1968, pp.58-63.

36   Some researches have been unable to 'separate' the influence of actual and ideal self-images on product preference and consumption as, for example, Hamm, B.C. and Cundiff, E.W. ('Self Actualisation and Product Perception', *Journal of Marketing Research,* November 1969, pp.470-2) who found women very aware of home, car and dress but found no significant difference between real-self and ideal-self product perceptions.

37   Stern, B.L., Bush, R.F., Hair, J.F., 'The Self-Image/Store Image Matching Process: An Empirical Test', *Journal of Business,* vol.50, 1977, pp.63-9.

38 See Packard, V., op.cit.—reference pp.117, 118.

39 Dolich, I.J., 'Congruence Relationships Between Self-Images and Product Brands', *Journal of Marketing,* February 1969, pp.80-4.

40 Kanti Prasad, V., 'Socioeconomic Product Risk and Patronage Preferences of Retail Shoppers', *Journal of Marketing Research,* vol.39, July 1975, pp.42-7.

41 Had the strategy not been successful, manufacturers would have quickly abandoned it as a part of their marketing planning.

42 Some volume dependent manufacturers have attempted to exploit this potentially lucrative market with a range of 'prestige' products sold at appropriately high prices. As a general rule they have met with very limited success and have found great difficulty in reconciling their mass market activities with attempts to project a high price, 'exclusive' image over a small part of their overall product range.

7 Perspective

Cross-cultural studies of conspicuous consumption do show that the nature and incidence of this exceptional form of behaviour are determined for the most part by social and economic environment.

Firstly, cultural 'approval' of ostentatious display appears to be a central factor in deciding a society's overall propensity to conspicuously consume and such behaviour is most in evidence in those communities which actively encourage and promote the display of material and pecuniary advantage as a means of securing social status. Cultural recognition and acceptance, however, can be conditional or unconditional. Approval in many of the more primitive traditional societies was given only when ostentatious economic display was channelled into socially acceptable forms and conspicuous consumption was clearly directed and controlled through a complex system of social custom, ritual and obligation. In contrast, the general public acceptance of 'Gilded Age' conspicuous consumption in the United States appears, for some considerable time at least, to have allowed any and all forms of ostentation and display.

The influence of specific sub-cultures also seems to be particularly strong and conspicuous consumption would appear to be most rewarding for those individuals who are not only members of a society whose dominant culture is sympathetic to such behaviour but who are also exposed to sub-cultural environments which actively encourage conspicuous display for purposes of status gain. When cultural and sub-cultural values are in conflict, however, behaviour would appear to be modified in the longer term to conform more closely with the wider social environment—more particularly, when ostentatious display is undertaken at significantly high levels of expenditure.

Social class influences on conspicuous consumption are difficult to measure but the evidence suggests that class based display competition, as and when it occurs, is predominantly 'horizontal' rather than 'vertical' in direction. Social class barriers may in fact suppress rather than encourage vertical status seeking conspicuous consumption. And whilst there is evidence to support Veblen's contention that conspicuous materialism is to be found to some extent in all social classes and at all social and economic levels in more traditional societies, it does not appear to be particularly predominant amongst the very rich and in the blue-collar working class groups found in modern post-Veblen industrialised nations.

With regard to reference groups, there is again sufficient evidence to show that ostentatious economic display directed at groups to which an individual 'refers' is tolerated within limits by all forms of social organisation. As expected, reference groups do seem to be of greater importance in shaping consumer behaviour in the affluent, developed societies and there is a good correlation between the relative rise in reference group influence on conspicuous consumption and the decline of ascribed social class as a major determinant of consumer aspirations and behaviour.

Finally, the study has drawn some conclusions with respect to the economics of conspicuous consumption. Absolute economic superiority has clearly allowed often outrageous levels of ostentatious display in the past—particularly when economic power was allied with political and industrial authority—but it is income and wealth relativities which determine individual opportunities to conspicuously consume at all points on the social and economic scale.

Notwithstanding the evidence which confirms that conspicuous consumption is primarily conditioned by social and economic environment, it is important not to understate the considerable differences which can exist between societies in so far as the motivation and opportunity to conspicuously consume are concerned. In fact, these differences are substantial enough to remove any hopes that it may be possible to develop a general theory of status directed consumer behaviour which would have universal application.

Primitive traditional communities were remarkable for their overall lack of what is commonly held to be 'pure' conspicuous consumption. Display behaviour was for the most part ritualistic and directed by long standing social convention. Conspicuous saving and the public redistribution of accumulated wealth had little in common with the ostentatious conspicuous display described and condemned by Veblen and only the phenomenon of conspicuous destruction would seem to have been motivated by the desire to flaunt material advantage and social status.

In contrast, the feudal societies which emerged later allowed a far greater degree of pure conspicuous display. In the earlier stages of feudalism the rulers and their immediate retinues enjoyed monopoly economic and political power and could squander the community's wealth in asserting their privilege and dominance. The later more complex stages of development, however, often required a more equitable spread of income and wealth to accommodate an increasing dependence on military and bureaucratic strategic elites who held the system together.

Traditional societies could and did take many contrasting forms but it is interesting to see that within most communities there was a recognised need for ritual conspicuous consumption at all levels and mechanisms existed to allow such display behaviour even amongst those who were socially and economically disadvantaged—most typically through conspicuous activities which were self-financing or through permitted display on certain social occasions (weddings and funerals, for example) which posed no threat to the ascribed social order. Consequently, conspicuous consumption could be seen at all levels of society and received broad approval within the community at large.

Within achieving societies, examination of the relevant periods of American and British social and economic history shows that the conservative ritual often associated with conspicuous consumption in anthropologically 'earlier' forms of community largely disappears. Conspicuous ostentatious display in the nineteenth century United States, for example, was aggressive—ascribed privilege was under attack as cultural and ethical changes combined to create an environment in which status could be increasingly awarded on the basis of achievement. In Britain, the ritual role of ostentatious display also ended but here the change of direction was perhaps less radical in that conspicuous consumption continued for the most part with the well entrenched ascribed status elites (financed when necessary by plutocrats with ascribed status ambitions) and was never taken up in great measure by the newly prosperous but socially deferential middle classes which emerged from the Industrial Revolution.

One point of interest to come from studies of nineteenth century American and British conspicuous consumption is that the ultimate objective of such behaviour in both societies during these years of radical social and economic change may well have been identical—namely, to secure and consolidate future ascribed status rather than to benefit from any immediate social recognition based on recent achievement. If such was the case (and present day social registers in both countries lend substantial support to the hypothesis) then achieving society display was—and is today—a good deal more conservative in social terms than has commonly been assumed and the distinction between conspicuous consumption in traditional and achieving societies becomes less clearly defined.

Finally, the nature of conspicuous consumption in today's affluent societies appears to diverge quite radically from such behaviour as it has been observed in earlier forms of social organisation. Perhaps the greatest single change lies in the fact that conspicuous consumption is 'managed' in volume production, consumer oriented societies to an extent far beyond anything seen before. In less sophisticated communities which were not geared to, or dependent on, mass production and distribution, the stimulus to ostentatious economic display was derived either from longstanding ritual or—in the achieving societies—from individual status seeking inspired by accumulated wealth. In contrast, any cultural or personal drives to conspicuously consume are modified or used in the consumer societies to generate demand for goods and services which are promoted to status seeking consumers as socially valuable products.

On the evidence of status directed consumption in traditional, achieving and affluent societies, therefore, a pattern of change emerges with respect to the nature and objectives of conspicuous consumption which parallels changes in the social and economic organisation of the communities themselves. Ascribed status goals dominate in the traditional social system and can persist through the transition to achieving society even though the conspicuous consumption observed in this later stage of social development appears at first sight to be strongly achievement oriented. In the consumer societies, however, ascribed status is clearly no longer to be 'purchased' through ostentatious display but conspicuous consumption itself survives and prospers under the stimulus of demand management which encourages individuals to consume for short term, achieved status gains.

The above conclusions are valid but must nevertheless be put in better perspective. For research purposes, it was felt necessary at the outset to identify and isolate three basic forms of social organisation for separate analysis. Dominant rather than exclusive social characteristics were taken to determine the classification of societies as traditional, achieving or affluent. Cultural, social and economic attitudes to conspicuous consumption were then examined within each distinct form of social organisation. Whilst this methodology was justified in that it allowed a necessary 'structure' to be given to the research frame, the implicit assumption of 'exclusive' social organisations (which do not in fact exist) limits its empirical value and can take us no further.

For the most part, nations and communities today have a mix of social characteristics and are able to accommodate individuals and families whose attitudes and cultural values can range from traditional to modern. Moreover, changes in society and in character type do not occur all at once and there is inevitably a considerable overlapping which means that it is possible, within one society, to find individuals and groups who 'date' metaphorically from different stages of economic and social development and who will have attitudes towards conspicuous consumption which are markedly different.

The mixing of people who have different cultural and social values comes most significantly from 'internal' factors—such as unequal regional development, wide variations in communication effectiveness and the inequitable allocation of economic resources—and from 'external' change agents linked to colonisation, migration and immigration. And the 'mix' can vary widely. Many countries in the Third World, for example, can still be seen to have predominantly traditional value systems which often co-exist with far smaller but rapidly growing achievement oriented sub-cultures developed by the new urban elites who may well have inherited their positions from former colonial or neo-colonial rulers. In contrast, the social organisation of North American and Western European nations is today dominated by affluent, consumer motivated attitudes which have already effectively reduced traditional values to those imported by more recent immigrant groups.

Although it is possible to observe wide variations in the mix of peoples and attitudes within any given society, the direction of change is invariably towards modern value systems and away from those norms associated with earlier more traditional forms of social organisation. Moreover, the pace of change is increasing rapidly as better communications bring more and more people into contact with the 'media philosophies' which have played a central role in changing attitudes and ideas. The nature of conspicuous consumption will therefore not only reflect the current mix of attitudes to ostentatious display in any society but will change as the mix itself changes over time; and we can expect the adoption of more consumer oriented values to bring about a corresponding shift in patterns of conspicuous display further away from ascribed ritual and towards induced achievement motivated status seeking within managed economies geared to the volume production of goods.

Whilst conspicuous consumption in its various forms can be observed today in a majority of societies throughout the world, one major exception or special case must be recognised. There are today a considerable number of modern socialist or state socialist nations which would claim that such behaviour has no place in their societies and that significant status directed conspicuous display in effect no longer exists for them. At the very least, there can be no doubt that in socialist countries the observed level of conspicuous consumption is minimal when compared with that of the more capitalist nations. To understand why this should be so, and to gain some insight into future developments, it is necessary to digress briefly and look at the principles and priorities of socialist society.

State socialism is, in theory at least, government by the people and for the people. Under Marxism-Leninism the political elite, acting for and on behalf of the people, defines and protects the value of the society. There is therefore a single universally applied value system which is claimed to serve the interests of the majority and any behaviour which is not politically condoned and legitimised is seen as an attack on this majority and represents anti-social self-interest. In particular, behaviour which seeks to heighten social class differences (seen as an unavoidable product of capitalist societies) is condemned out of hand. Social 'deviance' is therefore any departure from politically conditioned and expected rules of conduct—rules which are recognised as socially and morally legitimate within the society. In effect, socially deviant behaviour is politically deviant behaviour because under state socialism— as opposed to democratic socialism—the political elite defines all social values. And as the ultimate political ambition is to create a society of equals, deviations from the norm are reduced to a minimum.

The egalitarian aspirations of socialist societies can not, however, produce egalitarian systems of government. State socialism, like capitalism, has to be hierarchically organised. Firstly, as in all organised societies, there exists a political leadership charged with protecting the widest interest of the community and with furthering the socialist ideal. Membership of this political elite undoubtedly confers status and privileges on the individual and makes him decidedly 'unequal' with non-members.. Secondly, inequalities based on occupational differences are accepted and variations in rewards based on different levels of skills are legitimised by an ideology which argues that under socialism men give according to their ability and receive according to their work. It is accepted that some work is more valuable to society and that in practice some individuals perform more efficiently than others—both factors which justify differential rewards as functionally necessary to educational and economic advance. However, socialism departs from capitalism quite fundamentally by insisting that the resulting inequalities of power and income are not used to sharpen the conflict between individuals, between rich and poor and between the different social 'classes' which may still exist in the transitional stages of development.

Modern socialist states are therefore seeking to combine the social equality of the earliest traditional societies (whose cultural philosophy is often described as 'primitive communism') with a technological and economic efficiency which requires a hierarchical system of government and social organisation. To achieve these dual aims, any necessary inequalities in the system—whether political or economic—must be seen to profit only the community at large and must not allow individuals the right or opportunity to break ranks and proclaim their own economic or social superiority.

Given the egalitarian objectives of socialist societies and the commitment to removing all social class distinctions, individual conspicuous consumption is seen as a socially deviant form of behaviour. Conspicuous display is evident in capitalist societies, it is argued, because in the class conscious social conditions of bourgeois society, social relationships become reified into relations between things and not between people, and social status comes to be measured in terms not only of relative wealth but also of relative possessions. Social prestige therefore becomes dependent on objects rather than on interpersonal relations and the level of conflict within society is inevitably raised.

It follows that if conspicuous consumption is observed within avowedly socialist societies it serves to demonstrate that residual capitalist class values must still exist within a section of the community. In a sense, therefore, observed conspicuous consumption acts as an indicator of progress (or, more correctly, of lack of progress) towards the truly socialist state. Once socialism is achieved, individual conspicuous display will theoretically disappear as the motivation and stimuli necessary to conspicuous consumption are themselves eliminated within a classless communist society.

Looked at a little more objectively, it is not at all certain that the socialist interpretation of conspicuous consumption will prove to be correct. Firstly, while there can be no doubt that such behaviour prospers more easily in heavily stratified societies, there is no real evidence to show that it is particularly associated with social class stratification—indeed, the present study has shown that social class differences can act—and have acted—as barriers to vertical status seeking through conspicuous consumption. Similarly, there is again no evidence to indicate that occupational and educational elites—encouraged in the socialist system—will enjoy sufficient status conference to ignore opportunities to assert their corresponding income superiority; the capitalist experience of diploma elites suggests the opposite. In short, the strong, almost exclusive, correlation between conspicuous consumption and social class conflict which is implied in socialist philosophy would appear to be too simplistic and lacking in empirical support.

In predicting an end to their own conspicuous consumption, many advanced socialist states choose to contrast the far lower levels of ostentatious display which are already in evidence in their societies with those commonly observed in more democratic capitalist states. Again, it is not at all clear how and why these reduced levels of conspicuous consumption have been achieved; it is, in fact, difficult to decide whether the lower incidence is due to voluntary rejection of such consumption by individual members of the community or to the active suppression and condemnation of conspicuous economic display by the political elite. Any judgement on this issue runs a risk of being politically prejudiced but there can be no doubt that the substantially reduced levels of conspicuous consumption evident in socialist society have not been achieved under conditions of real consumer sovereignty and consequently can not be shown to have been voluntarily brought about. Only under free market conditions can any elimination of conspicuous consumption claim to have been publicly proposed rather than politically imposed.

Another explanation for low levels of conspicuous consumption lies in the fact that, for most if not all state socialist societies, investment capital has traditionally and ideologically been directed towards consolidating and expanding the industrial base rather than to developing the consumer goods sectors of the economy. To this extent, the individual consumer is often faced not only with shortages and rationing but with little or no product choice. Furthermore, consumer goods and services have been standardised and have offered no opportunity for individuals either to discriminate between products or to pay more, if they so wish, for a 'superior' good which confers status benefits. And when it is not possible for the consumer to discriminate between competing goods on the basis of price, then the opportunity (as opposed to the motivation) for conspicuous consumption effectively disappears.

Looking to the future, there are already signs that in the more developed and affluent socialist states the consumer is seeking a far greater selection and range of goods and services to be made available to him and that pressures are building up within the system for a more equitable spread of investment between industrial and consumer goods. As discretionary incomes grow and greater freedom of consumer choice is introduced into those economies the opportunity to conspicuously consume will grow pro rata.

In the medium term, demand pressures should increase the flow of basic foodstuffs and consumer durables which have traditionally been in short supply. These 'new' goods will be purchased for their direct utility value in making the quality of life more agreeable and acceptable. However, once these utility needs are met, a more critical phase will be reached in so far as conspicuous consumption is concerned. Under conditions of increasing individual affluence, Maslow's *Hierarchy of Needs* analysis would predict a further shift in the pattern of demand from physiological to psychological needs, creating demand pressures for goods which possess not only some functional utility value but also status attributes which are able to enhance individual prestige and self-esteem. Such predictions, however, contradict Marxist theory which implies that within socialist societies individuals will not be motivated to consume status goods and that such socio-psychological demand will be conspicuous only by its absence. Given the necessary freedom of expression and consumer choice, we can only wait and see which interpretation proves to be correct in the longer term and then perhaps reassess the relationship between conspicuous consumption and state socialism.

In concentrating for research purposes only on 'pure' conspicuous consumption—that is, on consumption which is overwhelmingly and self-evidently motivated by status considerations—the real impact and importance of status linked consumption in modern non-socialist societies is without doubt considerably understated.

Firstly, there are many purchases made today which are motivated primarily for the direct utility value they offer to the individual but which are also influenced in part by many conspicuous status linked attributes offered by the products themselves. Whilst it is not possible to measure the degree to which predominantly direct utility purchases are influenced by secondary considerations of status conference, a cursory review of product advertising and promotional campaigns is sufficient to demonstrate that a wide range of utility goods are made more attractive—and are more easily sold—by being linked to claims of potential status gains.

It is clearly in the interests of manufacturers to promote the social as well as the practical benefits of their products, as both these attributes can be charged to the consumer and passed on in higher prices. Furthermore, unlike functional utility, 'social engineering' in product management is a relatively low cost operation for the producer which can be achieved through appropriate advertising and packaging policies at little extra cost. For many years now, manufacturers have therefore broadened the appeal of utility goods by emphasising social attributes as secondary benefits available to the consumer and there is no reason to suppose that such business policies will not continue in the future for a wider range of commodities.

Unfortunately, the extent to which the social attributes of utility products are consciously 'purchased' by consumers can not be realistically assessed. In practice, there will inevitably be significant differences not only between purchasers and non-purchasers but also within purchasing groups themselves as to how important any secondary status linked considerations are in persuading them to buy a particular product. Notwithstanding the difficulties of measurement, however, it is necessary to recognise that there is often a disguised element of conspicuous consumption in many utility purchases and that this element increases substantially in the consumer oriented societies as status linked consumption is more effectively exploited.

In addition to the possibility of 'status purchasing' in the market for utility goods, overall levels of conspicuous consumption may also be understated for reasons which relate to consumer reactions to price and to price movements. There are certain circumstances in which consumers are considered to make 'rational' (i.e. economically justified) decisions to demand more of a product or service as its price is increased and again these decisions may disguise a significant element of conspicuous consumption.

Firstly, the 'expectations effect'. It is argued that peoples' purchasing behaviour at any point in time is determined not only by their present financial circumstances and by current market conditions but also by their expectations as to what the future will bring. Behaviour is seen to be strongly influenced by the individual's expectations as to his personal finances in the months or years ahead—any anticipated promotion or substantial salary increase, for example, causing him to revalue his current level of financial commitment and perhaps to spend and consume more. At the same time, he will have price expectations—that is, he will form a considered opinion as to future price trends, taking into account such factors as the rate of inflation, changes in market structure and competition, etc. and will adjust his expenditures accordingly.

If the consumer's view of the future rate of price increases is particularly pessimistic, it becomes more attractive for him to bring forward planned purchases of high price commodities and to buy the goods in question immediately even if current prices are already high. Consequently, in times of high inflation and considerable uncertainty as to the future, consumers have been observed to increase their purchases of certain commodities as prices themselves increase—behaviour which has the effect of producing notionally upward sloping demand curves over periods of time.

Whilst the price expectations effect may be considered the most convincing explanation for such positive demand/price correlations, it is also true that any increase in the price of a particular product makes that product potentially more attractive to the conspicuous consumer. It therefore follows that a part of the increased demand which is generated as prices rise may be 'conspicuous' demand which derives not from the expectations effect but from the relative increase in status conference which the new product is seen to offer to the consumer seeking social prestige in addition to direct functional utility. More simply, the price increase is seen to change the 'mix' of functional and social product attributes by increasing the product's status benefits in the eyes of the consumer.

Again, there is no satisfactory way in which disguised conspicuous consumption can be separated out from more 'rational' consumer reactions to anticipated price inflation, but it is reasonable to assume that trace elements of status purchasing will be included in many decisions to increase expenditures under such conditions. And if these trace elements exist, then conspicuous consumption, in aggregate, runs the risk of being underestimated.

The second price related factor which can effectively mask conspicuous buyer behaviour is concerned with the price-quality relationship which is implicit in many decisions to buy. It is generally accepted that the quality of a product in the eyes of the consumer is positively correlated with its price—that, other things being equal, the higher the price then the better the quality of the purchase. This relationship would appear to be particularly important in those circumstances when the buyer has little or no first-hand knowledge of the product or products he wishes to purchase and so has to fall back on price as a secondary indicator of the relative value of competing goods.

The price-quality association is once more able to produce notionally upward sloping demand curves for products about which consumers are particularly quality sensitive. Higher prices are taken to reflect better quality and can therefore generate increased demand. Given the assumption on which these consumers are basing their purchase decisions, such behaviour is 'rational' and consistent but, again, high prices can not only suggest better quality but can also increase the status value of products and it is possible that any increase in demand at relatively high price levels includes an element of conspicuous consumption which is intended to profit from the potential status gains made from 'expensive' purchases.

While it is not possible to measure the extent to which high price consumption attributed to the price-quality relationship masks conspicuous purchasing behaviour, there is a real possibility that a significant amount of conspicuous consumption goes unrecognised. The result, once again, is that in concentrating on 'pure' conspicuous consumption, the real incidence of status linked purchasing may be considerably understated. At the very least, given the opportunities for disguised conspicuous display through both the expectations effect and the price-quality association, errors in measurement will always tend to understate rather than exaggerate the overall importance of ostentatious consumption.

Finally, another factor needs to be recognised which also makes it possible to significantly underestimate the overall incidence and importance of conspicuous economic display. This study has focused exclusively on those environmental factors which motivate individuals to conspicuously consume and allow them the opportunity to behave in this way. What has not been examined in any detail is the phenomenon of group conspicuous display and the conspicuous consumption of organisations rather than of individuals.

It has already been noted that in the more traditional and feudal societies, the church, for example, was (and is) a conspicuous consumer of some significance and that a considerable amount of individual discretionary income has been channelled into religious display of one form or another. In one sense, such ostentation may not qualify as pure conspicuous consumption because it can be seen not as pure display expenditure but as a duty of the church and as both a duty and an 'investment' by the many individuals who contribute to such activity. Nevertheless, it remains true that in many present day traditional societies, or societies in which traditional value systems have endured, religious display is perhaps the most recognisable—and often the most accepted and acceptable—form of conspicuous consumption.

Many dissenting religious groups came into being partly to oppose the waste and idolatry of the older more traditional faiths and in those countries which have become predominantly Protestant the incidence of such behaviour is much reduced—indeed, a conscious policy of 'conspicuous reserve' is often adopted by religious leaders and by their congregations. Consequently, it is possible to observe very wide variations in the levels of conspicuous religious consumption within and between individual nations; as a general rule, the more traditional the church, the greater the level of conspicuous behaviour. In those countries where significant levels of religious display are condoned and even expected, however, the overall incidence of conspicuous consumption is much increased by the activities of the church.

Two other forms of 'organised' conspicuous consumption also need to be acknowledged, for both are much in evidence in the modern world. Firstly, the creation of many new nation-states in the last twenty to thirty years has encouraged a phenomenon which is perhaps best described as 'state conspicuous consumption'. New nations often feel the need to establish and proclaim their separate identity and independence and many governments have resorted to conspicuous display as a suitable means of affirming their existence, authority and ambitions. Levels of state conspicuous consumption (or state 'waste', as its critics would argue) can reach major proportions and have been known to consume a sizeable part of a nation's gross national product at times when the need for investment in economic and social development should have had a prior claim on available resources. As a result, independence arches and other prestige projects are in evidence throughout the greater part of the developing world.

State conspicuous consumption is, of course, not the sole preserve of newly independent nations. The need for international status and recognition has also prompted investment in conspicuous prestige expenditures in most modern industrialised societies. Moreover, such consumption cuts across all political philosophies and occurs in both capitalist and socialist countries; indeed, the importance and prestige of the state in many socialist countries actively encourages the diversion of display capital away from the individual and towards the central authority which may then conspicuously consume for and on behalf of the nation.

As with religious display, it can be argued that state ostentation does not qualify as pure conspicuous consumption and that there is a clear need for countries to establish, consolidate and improve their image not only at home but abroad. Apologists for such consumption would argue firstly that newly established nations need to establish an identity in order to produce a greater commitment to work and public service amongst their own citizens and perhaps to make the population more prepared to face short or medium term deprivation in the nation's long term interest. Secondly, state conspicuous consumption is seen as necessary in international terms as levels of economic and social interdependence continue to increase and as trading partners are often judged by their apparent wealth and financial status.

If these arguments can be accepted—and most observers would concede that there is often an unquantifiable utility value in such consumption—then state display cannot be held to be pure conspicuous consumption as it has been defined in this work. At the same time, there is without much doubt a considerable element of conspicuous waste in these state expenditures which is more properly seen as Veblenian conspicuous consumption, intended primarily for national status raising rather than as a stimulus to productivity and wealth creation. Whilst it is not possible to differentiate between pure status display and the utility element in state consumption, it is reasonable to conclude that most conspicuous consumption of this type contains both elements to some degree. And to the extent that state consumption is ignored or discounted in any study of ostentatious display, then levels of conspicuous consumption calculated solely on the basis of observed 'individual' behaviour can seriously understate the overall intensity and importance of such consumption. This will be particularly true for those countries which may actively suppress individual status directed expenditures but which may indulge in quite considerable levels of state controlled conspicuous display.

Finally, and in addition to the increase in state conspicuous consumption which has been a feature of more recent years, the affluent mixed economy nations of the West have witnessed the growth of yet another form of organised conspicuous display which has largely come into being as a direct result of the substantial economic and political changes which accompany the transition from developing to industrial and post-industrial society.

It has already been noted that, in moving away from achieving society values and towards the more consumer oriented norms of the fully industrialised society, the economic and political authority of the individual entrepreneur is rapidly eroded. This loss of personal power and prestige has historically been accompanied by a corresponding reduction in levels of plutocratic conspicuous consumption but as wealth and power shift away from the individual it spawns a new variation of ostentatious display—the conspicuous consumption of business corporations themselves.

'Corporate conspicuous consumption' is today very much in evidence and operates at two levels. Firstly, the status of the corporation is held to be a matter of very great concern and importance and substantial sums are spent in ensuring that the company does not lack for public prestige and esteem. Secondly, individual company employees conspicuously consume in efforts to satisfy a need for highly visible signs of

148

authority. The result is that the directors and managers of many corporations 'are trained in the nuances of status and systematise the apportioning of perks'.

Once again, corporate conspicuous consumption can be seen as an investment rather than as pure display expenditure intended to secure status only through revealed wealth. Company image—particularly in terms of perceived financial strength—can have a pronounced effect on public acceptance and on corporate ambitions in the capital market. Consumer reaction to any branded product or service is similarly determined in part by buyer perception of the manufacturing company or of the supplier and so expenditure intended to reinforce or improve corporate standing and reputation can be taken as necessary rather than wasteful spending and can make a significant contribution to sales effectiveness and ultimately to profitability. Finally, there is little doubt that many company employees—more especially in the managerial ranks—respond positively to the status incentives which have come to play a central role in many aspects of corporate personnel management.

Whilst accepting many of the arguments which justify corporate 'investment' in status seeking both inside and outside the organisation, it is again reasonable to assume that such behaviour will contain a substantial—if officially hidden—element of pure conspicuous consumption and that the activities of corporations as status directed consumers add considerably to the total incidence of conspicuous consumption within any industrialised society. Once more, too great a preoccupation with individual display can lead to results which ignore the importance of conspicuous consumption in its 'corporate' form.

This study of conspicuous consumption has necessarily focused on the incidence of such behaviour as it has been observed in traditional and modern societies both past and present. It is worth concluding, however, by looking briefly to the future and to ways in which the nature and direction of status linked consumption may change in the post-affluence stages of social and economic development.

Some observers now believe that the other-directed materialism of affluent societies will not be sustained in future years and that there will be a substantial reassessment of attitudes and values within consumer oriented societies. In particular, it is predicted that the display of material superiority which has to date been actively encouraged by the 'admass' culture will become increasingly unacceptable within society and that, ultimately, personal status and prestige will cease to be a motivating force of any real significance in directing consumer behaviour.

In support of these claims, there is already evidence to show that the very rich in affluent societies, for reasons already explained in the previous chapter, have come to reject ostentatious display as a means to status consolidation and improvement—indeed, they now often take pains to be particularly inconspicuous in their expenditures, consumption and lifestyles. Secondly, status directed conspicuous consumption within the so-called working class—a phenomenon which once served a strong ritual role—is no longer a force in determining patterns of consumer behaviour. As a result, conspicuous consumption may well be confirmed in future as an exclusively 'middle class' form of behaviour, finding acceptance and being considered a rewarding activity only by those who see themselves at or about the middle of the social hierarchy and who are consequently highly susceptible to status dominated appeals and opportunities.

Given present trends, the argument that conspicuous consumption will increasingly be confined within a middle class 'redoubt' is convincing; certainly it is difficult to believe either that it will regain its status appeal with the very rich in post-industrial societies or that it will undergo a renaissance and again become as powerful and important as it can be in societies which are moving through highly achievement-oriented stages of their economic and social development. Moreover, whilst any expectations of a major resurgence in such behaviour are widely discounted, there are those who would argue further that conspicuous consumption will not survive in the longer term even within the broad middle class itself as cultural and social values are inevitably reassessed and revised.

The previous chapter showed that conspicuous consumption in the affluent societies continues to flourish firstly because the occupational and educational elites find it necessary to express their status superiority in a socially visible form and secondly because lower middle class consumers are able to 'disguise' educational and occupational shortcomings by adopting conspicuous lifestyles which imitate those of the professional middle class. In essence, therefore, conspicuous consumption feeds off a status system which lays great emphasis on individual achievement but which has to allow surrogate indicators to be used in asserting claims to status. For as long as occupation and education continue to dominate status conference then conspicuous consumption should prosper, but many observers now believe that these two 'achievements' will come to play a far less important role in deciding social standing and prestige in the later stages of post-industrial society.

There are already signs in the affluent nations that the respect paid to those who enjoy occupational and educational status is rapidly eroding and that these societies are undergoing a process of cultural and social change which will accentuate rather than arrest this erosion. Established middle class values, for example, are now seen to be under increasing pressure and the class itself may be losing the cachet it once enjoyed. In part, conspicuous consumption has itself contributed to this trend by giving opportunities for status advance to those whom the 'real' middle class see as status inferiors and many of the diploma elites now feel the class to be 'an amorphous, undistinguished mass, adulterated by a flood of new entrants from below who have effectively degraded class values and obscured class boundaries' (Anon).

The post-industrial middle class is in many ways better defined as the 'managerial class'—a term which implicitly places far less emphasis on professional occupation and on educational excellence and which can more easily accommodate lower middle class individuals and their aspirations. As and when this new managerial class succeeds in redefining 'status' in modern societies, it is argued, so conspicuous consumption will itself come under greater pressure. Firstly, the professional middle class will see no advantage in attempting to emphasise their assumed superiority by seeking to display a level of wealth which—as a result of the marked narrowing of income gaps—can no longer be taken to reflect their occupational and educational achievements. Secondly, the new class structure, by accommodating aspiring 'new entrants' regardless of background or education, will effectively remove their need to conspicuously consume and will channel status expenditure and consumption in new directions.

If these predictions of future social and economic change prove to be correct, then the importance and incidence of conspicuous consumption, other things being equal, should certainly decline. However, whilst present social trends may point in this direction, the situation is in reality far more complex. It has already been seen that conspicuous consumption has historically shown a remarkable capacity to survive social and political change. It adapts to new conditions and seems to be able to find a new raison d'etre which justifies its continuing existence at some level and with some individuals in nearly all societies. Moreover, the need of modern industry and commerce to general volume demand for an ever increasing range of socially visible consumer goods will certainly put pressure on governments and manufacturers to support and perhaps even to strengthen the links between status aspirations and consumption—links which have been shown to stimulate high levels of demand for conspicuous products. It is entirely possible, therefore, that conspicuous consumption will survive the transition from affluent consumer oriented societies partly through its own proven ability to find some justifications within any social system and partly as a result of being valued and 'managed' by commercial groups who will have a vested interest in seeing it prosper.

There are already signs of a developing conflict between cultural rejection of status directed material display and the political and industrial dependence on such behaviour in affluent freely organised societies. At this time it is not at all certain how the conflict will be resolved, but the history and development of conspicuous consumption to date suggests that it will endure to some greater or lesser extent as an expression of personal and social identity in an increasingly uniform world.

Index

development, 18
traits, 27
and ostentatious display, 26-7
Phillips, D.G., 98n
Plutocracy, 89-90
Poole, E., 98n
population, growth and distribution, 36
potlatch ceremonies, 49-50
prices, 2, 120, 121, 144-6
expectations effect, 145
and product-quality, 145-6
primitive communism, 48
Prince of Wales, 89
product positioning, 121

Rae, J., 3-4, 15n, 17, 19
Ramsey, P., 99n
ratchet effect, on conspicuous consumption, 69, 76
Ratner, S., 97n
reciprocal entertaining, 61
Reeve, A.B., 98n
reference groups, 24-5
Reform Bill (1832), 84, 99n, 100n
Regency, 82-3
research methodology, 42-5
retailers, 118, 122
revealed taste, 108-9, 110, 116, 120
Rex, J., 34n
Riesman, D.A., 14n, 45n, 131n
Riis, J., 98n
Rischin, M., 97n
Roberts, K., 133n
Robertson, R.T., 134n
Rockefeller, 78, 132n
Roeber, A.L., 32n
Rome, 57
Roosevelt, 78
Ross, I., 134n
Routh, G., 133n
Rubel, M., 33n
Runciman, W.G., 33n

Saarinen, A.B., 96n
Sage, R., 98n
Sahlius, M.D., 65n
Salisbury, R.F., 66n
Sampson, A., 32n
Schlesinger, A.M., 98n
Seaman, L.C.B., 99n
self-help, 71-3, 75-6, 90, 97n
self-image, and consumption, 125-6
Semeonoff, E., 133n
Shanks, M., 32n
Shearman, T.G., 97n
Siane, 66n
Simond, L., 99n
Skotheim, R.A., 96n
Smiles, Samuel, 97n, 72
Smith, Adam, 2-3, 14n, 15n, 17, 20, 26
Smuts, R.W., 98n
snob effect, 128
market, 128-30
social character, 37-41
social class, 22
and conspicuous consumption, 23-4
social engineering, 121, 144
social obsolescence, in products, 122
social registers, 76, 79, 95
social stratification, and consumption, 30-1
socialisation, 103
Society of Mayfair Descendants, 75
Sons of American Revolution, 75
Sons of the Revolution, 75
Stafford, J.E., 134n
state conspicuous consumption, 147-8
state socialism:
ideology, 141
and conspicuous consumption, 141-3
status:

achieved, 39, 67-8, 85, 95-6
ascribed, 38, 52, 58, 95-6
status revolution, era of, 73
Stern, B.L., 133n, 134n
strategic elites, 31, 56, 58, 138
stratification:
social and economic, 30-1
and conspicuous consumption, 31
Strumpel, B., 132n
Strutts, 88
sub-cultures, 20-1
and conspicuous consumption, 21-2
Sullivan, H.S., 32n
sumptuary laws, 1, 57, 66n
Swazi, 65n

Tallensi, 64n
Tanala, 64n
taxation, 54
Ter Hoeven, P.J.A., 132n
Thibaut, J.W., 33n
Thoreau, H.D., 72, 75, 97n
Thouless, R.H., 32n, 33n
Tikopia, 64n
Titmuss, R.M., 33n
Tlingit, 50
traditional society, 20, 37-8
Trobriand Islanders, 51, 64n
Tsimshian, 50
Tylor, E.B., 32n

Vanity, 4
and personality, 18-19
vaygua, 64n
Veblen, Thorstein, 1, 5-12, 13, 15n, 17, 19, 20, 23, 26, 52, 98n, 103, 131n, 137
Veblen effect, 17, 20
Venkatesan, M., 134n

Wallace, B.J., 64n
want creation, 115
Warner, Charles, 75
Warner, W.L., 32n, 34n, 132n
Washington Irving, 72
wealth:
and status, 6-12
and consumption, 28-30
Weber, M., 32n, 33n
Weiss, R., 97n
welfare state, 106
Weyl, W.E., 98n, 77
Whyte, W.F., 132n
Whyte, W.H., 133n
Willmott, P., 32n, 133n
Witt, R.E., 133n
Wohl, R.R., 97n
working class, and conspicuous consumption, 60-2, 80, 111-2

Yamey, B.S., 63n
Young, M., 32n, 133n

Zahn, E., 132n